Break Forth

To Kristen

♡ *Calli*

Break Forth

Becoming victorious over a past of abuse, trauma and domestic violence

Calli J. Linwood

Break Forth

Copyright ©2017 Calli J. Linwood

All rights reserved.

No part of this publication may be reproduced, stored in a retrieval system, or transmitted in any form by any process—electronic, mechanical, photocopying, recording, or otherwise—without prior written permission of the copyright owners and Ahelia Publishing, LLC. Any scanning, uploading, and distribution of this book via the Internet or any other means without the permission of the publisher is illegal and punishable by law.

Unless otherwise indicated, are taken from the HOLY BIBLE, NEW LIVING TRANSLATION (NLT): Scriptures taken from the HOLY BIBLE, NEW LIVING TRANSLATION, Copyright© 1996, 2004, 2007 by Tyndale House Foundation. Used by permission of Tyndale House Publishers, Inc., Carol Stream, Illinois 60188. All rights reserved. Used by permission.

All journal entries and appendix articles are taken directly, as they were written, from the author's personal journals. All names and locations have been changed to protect the privacy of individuals.

ISBN# 978-1-988001-11-1

Published by Ahelia Publishing, LLC
Printed in the United States of America
www.aheliapublishing.com
aheliapublishing@outlook.com

To Contact Calli directly, email her at cjlinwood@outlook.com

Other Books By Calli

Walking Tall

Watch for Calli's Upcoming release:

Coming Through the Fire

Justice will rule in the wilderness and righteousness in the fertile field. And this righteousness will bring peace. Yes, it will bring quietness and confidence forever. My people will live in safety, quietly at home. They will be at rest.
Isaiah 32:16-18

Therefore this is what the Sovereign Lord says: I will surely judge between the fat sheep and the scrawny sheep. For you fat sheep pushed and butted and crowded my sick and hungry flock until you scattered them to distant lands. So I will rescue my flock and they will no longer be abused.
Ezekiel 34:20-22

[God was there, even in the worst of it.]

Journal Entry - Spring, 2007

I just want to turn my head off for a while and stop the thoughts that are swirling around me, bombarding my heart & soul & mind & spirit.

"Be at peace, My child."

God, I can't keep living this, over and over again until I wind up in that unmentionable place where the only sensation I have is the pain that makes me want to lash out, to slash, to crash & burn and cry out in the night. "My God, where are You!? I can't do this alone."

"You are not alone, My child."

I need your peace, O Lord. Be still my mind and my heart.

Prophetic word – January, 2014

I kept seeing … break forth, break forth, break forth. Just that God is going to do such a break forth in you; that you are going to break forth, and that you are going to come with such freedom…

Prophetic word – October, 2014

I feel that within you there is that cry that is so loud and so incredibly desperate—that it is yelling "Freedom!" You have such a desire for freedom and you are surrendered, and you want to be free. And I see you running. I see you running through this really high grass, and it is really hard to run through. It is frustrating because it is hard to get through, but as you are getting faster and faster, all of a sudden you have this machete or something, and you are cutting down grass and it is getting faster and faster. You are getting the tools you need, and you are cutting it down, and before you know it, there is no grass there, and there is nothing in front of you and you are free. And all of a sudden, you are dancing around, and you are just free.

Contents

Introduction

Part One - My Healing Journey

1. Why We Go Back	....	Pg. 14
2. Walking with My Head Down	....	Pg. 16
3. Healing from Addictions	....	Pg. 28
4. Drowning Out Bitter Roots	....	Pg. 37
5. Hidden Jealousy	....	Pg. 49
6. Being Devoured	....	Pg. 59
7. The Letters on My Forehead	....	Pg. 75
8. The Shroud of Death	....	Pg. 85
9. Unheard Apology	....	Pg. 94

Part Two – Spiritual Development

10. Do My Prayer's Matter? .... Pg. 97

11. Life Changing Words .... Pg. 107

12. Praying for Your Enemies .... Pg. 117

13. The Most Amazing Horrible Day …. Pg. 127

14. Just Another Chapter .... Pg. 137

15. The Chains of Slavery .... Pg. 153

16. God's Protection .... Pg. 164

17. The Gift of Struggle .... Pg. 178

Appendix .... Pg. 188

A Final Word .... Pg. 190

End Notes and References .... Pg. 192

Coming Through the Fire–Prologue ….. Pg. 193

About the Author .... Pg. 195

Dear Reader,

If you've read Book One, *Walking Tall*,[1] then this book needs no introduction, except to say, "Welcome back!" I trust you have received some healing, or God would not have put my book in your hands once again. The story I have begun to tell you is not over. No, it is far from over. Like *Walking Tall*, it doesn't follow a sequential time line; both books are somewhat intermingled. In this book, we will continue to walk together through some areas of healing you may still need in order to become victorious over your past of abuse and trauma. Then we will deal with some further areas of your life to help you Break Forth into the abundant life God intended you to have. This is a hard walk, but the journey as a whole is amazing, and the freedom you will receive is so worth facing the pain. Often, the decision to face your pain and to take the first step are by far the hardest parts. Trust me, this I know!

If you are coming from a past of abuse and have not read *Walking Tall*, I highly recommend you start there. That book describes my journey of getting into, living in, staying in, leaving, and picking up the pieces from an abusive marriage, and how God set me on the right path to healing. It provides insight into the nature and dynamics of abusive relationships and exposes the reality of life in that situation. I shared my healing journey through my journals and my experiences, and I guide the reader through specific prayers to bring healing into their own lives. It is definitely more graphic than this book, but it was necessary for the context of telling the raw truth of my story.

I am honored you have chosen to allow me to walk this painful road with you, and I am proud of you for taking the risk of going after God to receive your own healing. I trust the Lord will bring further hope, health, peace and joy to your life through the pages and prayers of this book so you too, will walk in victory.

As you come to the end of each healing and teaching section, you will find a prayer. I did not write these prayers; I only edited them. They are Holy Spirit led and God breathed. The Lord carefully and precisely fashioned each prayer team and prayer time, leading us to pray in a way that reflected His heart for you. Pray these prayers out loud in a safe place, where you can allow the emotion and pain to flow freely, if need be. It is God's heart to heal you, but healing often comes with the pain of release, and the pain of birthing something new. Allow yourself the freedom and grace to walk through the pain, so you can receive the healing that comes on its heels.

It is in the prayers that Holy Spirit power of this book is released, and healing can come. The choice is yours. I urge you to take a stand and fight for the entire restoration of your body, soul and spirit. You do your part, and I guarantee the Lord will do *more* than His part. I will stand with you through it all, eagerly awaiting your story of how you were once a captive, set free by the love of the Lord, and His mercy and grace.

I give the prayer team a huge, heart felt thank-you for standing with me in this project. It was an honor to work with you. Your connection to Holy Spirit in your prayers will bring healing to many people. You are truly a blessing to me and to all the readers.

I want to give a special thank-you to Laura-Lynn Tyler Thompson,[2] without whom "The Hidden Chapter," in *Walking Tall* would still have been hidden. Your selfless obedience in fully exposing your heart in such a vulnerable area helped me to bare my own. I was so blessed to have met you so I could tell you my story in person.

The names of the parties involved, including my own, have once again been omitted or changed to protect privacy.

God bless, and love in Christ,

♥ *Calli J. Linwood*

> Publish his glorious deeds
> among the nations.
> Tell everyone about the amazing
> things he does.
> *1 Chronicles 16:24*

Journal Entry [one year, twelve days before I left the final time.]

March 5, 2007

"Just breathe…" Those are the words he related to as he watched his dad die. He could not "just breathe" anymore. How ironic that I'm in that place again, where I find it hard just to breathe; that I have to concentrate in order to breathe. That is my life. "Letting someone in again" this morning, it's all coming back; the swirling thoughts that won't stop, being numb, and just living through and not facing all that is happening. Just taking things as they happen, and not really thinking … is easier … but I know it is time. And this time there is so much more at stake … two little lives … two smiling, trusting faces … and so my journey begins.

[AGAIN … as I had let my mind and heart shut down for the last few years in order to just survive …]

Step one – Get out of the dark and be accountable. Talked to a counselor through the church. Will be accountable to her for my spiritual journey.
Step two – Get closer to God

Part One

My Healing Journey

For the LORD has redeemed Israel from those too strong for them. They will come home and sing songs of joy on the heights of Jerusalem. They will be radiant because of the LORD'S good gifts—the abundant crops of grain, new wine, and olive oil, and the healthy flocks and herds. Their life will be like a watered garden, and all their sorrows will be gone. The young women will dance for joy, and the men—old and young—will join in the celebration. I will turn their mourning into joy. I will comfort them and exchange their sorrow for rejoicing.
Jeremiah 31:11-13

Chapter One

Why We Go Back

*I*T'S HORRIBLY PAINFUL TO STAY IN A RELATIONSHIP THAT DEGRADES and disintegrates you. Yet, it is even more painful to leave. That is what outsiders do not understand. Upon leaving, the pain does not lessen. You still feel torn and broken. Confusion reigns; love and hate still battle to get the upper hand. The pieces of you are still lost, confidence still shattered, hope still gone. Only now, you have added to your life a multitude of complex problems with seemingly no solutions. Basic survival is daunting. Lack of finances and mounting debt overwhelm. Sorting through legal requirements unknown to you, force tears of frustration. Trying to soothe the heartbreak of your kids, while your own heart is raw and bleeding, feels impossible. And that is just the tip of all you have to walk through when you leave. And all the while, you still have to endure the constant nasty attacks of your abuser accusing you of being the evil one.

Break Forth

Though you are no longer in the same house, these tirades still can come hard and fast—sometimes even worse than before, as he frantically tries to reclaim all he believes is his, as it slowly slips from his grasp.

Looking over your shoulder to see if he is there is not a whole lot different than knowing he is. What we live when we leave is sometimes worse than what we lived. In that fragile state of mind, it is hard not to succumb to the promising lies that this time, it will be different. So we go back … again and again.

But what the insider does not understand in this broken state of mind is that if she can just hang on a little bit longer, a little bit longer, a little bit longer … healing will come. Going back to a broken vow without a complete healing of the relationship condemns her to a life that never was and will never be; the love and happiness she has ached for still will not be there. So though the pain is almost more than she can bear, she needs to understand it is temporary; things do change as healing comes, the light will come back into her eyes, and she will once again be free to think and feel and dance and breathe. And that is so worth it. And then she will know … then she will know she cannot go back.

Chapter Two

Walking with My Head Down

Journal Entry after less than one year of Marriage

June 25, 1999

    Today, well this morning at 1:30 a.m., was the third incident of what they call "low level" violence. My friends & family are scared to call. So today I start writing. He can't find this, but what do I have to lose? I feel trapped. Nothing I do is right. Not just the big things, but the little things too. I wash the floors, there's water spots. I use the wrong t-tow-

Break Forth

el. I cleaned the whole house (I had report cards to do, an assignment and a final exam) but my closet is a mess. I don't walk right, talk right, eat right, dress right, put my fork & knife on the plate when done eating right. I wear too much make-up, and my hair is not right. I am too busy (I agree with that.) I think that I am better than him. I look down on him because of his profession. I am stupid, naive, and I am terrible with money. I spend way too much. I hide money and lie about it. I think my business is a real business, but I should quit because I'm losing money. I should quit university, since I don't have the money. I shouldn't do any coaching or extra curricular, but only work 9:00-3:30. I should not help my friends with things unless I get paid. I shouldn't play soccer if it means I will not be in bed by 10:00. I have to be home for supper, unless it's university, and in bed by 10:00. I cannot go out without my husband. I am always putting myself in "compromising" situations, partying with married men, drinking & driving. I can't hang out with separated or single girls, or overweight people. I have contributed nothing in the decisions of the house. He does all the work. I am a pig, disrespectful, always fighting him, too independent. I want to do whatever the hell I want. I am going to get him & myself a bad reputation because I come in past 10:00, and

Break Forth

people will think he can't control his wife. All the other wives on our block just stay home & be housewives, and would not dare do anything without their husbands. Oh yeah, I am a b****, slut, whore and tramp. I am spiteful, and everything I do is calculating and manipulative. I am always trying to one up him and slam him. Anything that happens between our walls should stay between us, as no one else cares about us or our relationship. Our families have their own problems, and don't want to concern themselves with us. My friends won't be there for me; they just want to break up my marriage. I am deceitful, and full of lies. Oh yeah, I am a slob, my butt is as big as a house, and my family is uncultured. He never wanted to marry me; I pushed him into it. I don't appreciate the castle he built for me and/or the ring he bought for me. I don't wear my rings to the beach or soccer, so I don't want to be married. Everything I do is a game and disrespectful to him. I continually dismiss him & treat him like a hired hand. I don't care about him, and I don't write personal notes in the 'no occasion' cards I give him. I think I'm wonderful because I teach, what is it, brain surgery? I think I'm so great and that he has no life because I want to do things during the week/or summer holidays. I don't

Break Forth

give him the love & support he needs. I am embarrassed by him. I am a half-breed gypsy-sh**.

This is what my husband thinks of me. I do everything to push his buttons. I deserve whatever he gives me, as I provoke him and his violent reaction is what I deserve, and a normal reaction. I was the one who broke the trust. This is what my husband thinks of me.

I took a survey in a book the other day, and answering as leniently as possible, I was off the scale in emotional abuse, both isolation and degradation. Maybe it's time I admit I'm in an abusive relationship. I take responsibility for my part in it. I know I don't always put him first, but it is hard to put someone first that is always calling you down, saying how stupid you are and flipping out about things I really didn't think he would flip out about ...

I found this journal a month or so after I wrote *Walking Tall*. I forgot it even existed. There were no other entries in the whole journal. Though this entry went on for several more pages, it stopped mid-sentence. I can't remember why. It would be a little over a year before I would buy another journal (a Winnie-the-Pooh day planner so it would be inconspicuous and innocent), and begin writing again. Though I don't remember the specifics, I know we would have cycled through the abuse many more times in that year, repeating the same unending circle of abuse and honeymoon periods, while continually spiraling downwards.

I know the resources call it a cycle of abuse, but that does not fully explain the complex dynamics within the cycle. The cycle itself repeats again and again and again, but at the same time, over the years, the abuse and the abuser escalate—have to escalate—as the tolerance and numbness in both parties increase. The words cut deeper, the gestures are more threatening, physical violence can start, or its severity escalates. The noose of control gets tighter; more pressure to conform and perform is exerted. Higher levels of anger from the abuser lead to higher levels of fear in the victim. All the while we, the victims, are spiraling quickly downward. The walls around us grow thicker, tighter, blacker … crushing us.

The over stimulated adrenal glands and excessive cortisol constantly pumping though our bodies take their toll. Terror, anger, sadness, loneliness, isolation, desperation, hopelessness, despair and disillusionment take over our lives. Then, worn out and beyond exhausted, we go into shock and begin to shut down mentally, emotionally, spiritually, and physically with each horrific revolution of the cycle. We can tolerate an inhumane amount of abuse because of the numbness and shock, but eventually we get to the point where we are barely surviving, and definitely not living. We can become almost dead inside, only rallying enough to squeak out every physical thing he demands, and to keep on our false front to the public we mistakenly believe is protecting us. But at that point, we feel totally trapped and unable to see a way out. We have been disappointed so many times that we are scared to let hope in our hearts. If we start dreaming again it is eventually all crushed, and there we are, trying to pick ourselves up off the floor again and start over, each time with less hope, more fear, more wounds, less energy, more troubles pitted against us …

Break Forth

All these years later, and I still fell heavy just reading through my journey, recalling what was once my life. Now you try. Go back and read the journal entry again … and again … and again. And thus, you can easily understand how the spirit of heaviness has an open door, and can be set firmly in place in toxic relationships. But shutting down, isolating and pretending all is well is not the God intended response to the spirit of heaviness. Though we feel so weighted down we may believe that is all we are capable of, this is only what the enemy wants us to think. God has a much better option! This is what I learned, and this is how He showed me!

Casting off the Cloak of Heaviness

Words unsaid, my friend knew I carried a cloak of heaviness on my shoulders as I entered the church service that night. Whether it was my own past trauma stirred up in the Healing Shame seminar from that afternoon, or a burden from someone else, I still do not know. Though unlearned as yet by me, my friend knew this heaviness could only be broken through worship. She kept a watchful eye on me as the band played, to ensure I was doing my part. Before the end of praise and worship, I felt something suddenly break over me. I wept, and the heaviness lifted. God was definitely faithful in doing His part.

It was only later that I found out God had done more of His part than I had realized at the time. As the man, unknown to both my friend and me, approached us after the service and shared his story, I began to understand how intentional God is in training us. This man told us he had walked into church that evening, and had sat down on the far side. But God had said, "NO, over there." As he moved to our side of the sanctuary and sat several

Break Forth

rows behind us, God told him to worship over those two girls (my friend and me), and in particular, over that one (me). God knew what it would take to break the oppression over me, though at the time I did not.

This man was obedient in his assignment to worship over me. But I too, had to stop focusing on the weight that kept me hunched over, raise my hands and put my eyes and thoughts on Jesus. I had to give Him my adoration for who He was and for what He had done for me, even though it was a fight to do this because of the veil that shrouded me. I did not "feel like" raising my hands to Him, and it took a deliberate effort to do so. I definitely did not feel like worshipping at all. But worship I did, and in doing so, God not only freed me from the cloak of heaviness at that moment, but He also gave me the clear understanding and faith that the key to unlocking the heaviness in this life is to abandon all that weighs us down … no matter what it is, or how heavy it seems, and give Him the praise and worship that is due His name. By lifting Him up in spirit and in truth, we ourselves are lifted up out of the pit of despair, out of our desperation, turmoil and hopelessness, and set down, solid and steady, with a new song.

No matter what you are going through, dear Reader, no matter how heavy it feels, no matter how hard the fight, fight you must. Break through the barrier and worship Jesus. Raise your arms up to Him in praise. By lifting Him, He will lift you. That is always how it works. And it will work. By raising your arms you are praising Him, but you are also opening yourself up to receive what He has for you. You are inviting Him to come fill you up, and you are telling Him you trust Him enough to let Him come and pick you up. The Lord is a gentleman, and He will not force anything on you, even your own healing. You have to receive it. By keeping your arms tightly held into yourself, you may feel as if it is protecting you from being exposed and vulnerable, and thus keeping you from further harm. But I believe this keeps you

Break Forth

shut down and in a position—physically, mentally, emotionally and spiritually—where you cannot receive anything; any healing or any relief from the spirit of heaviness that plagues you.

This I know, as I held this posture of being curled in on myself for many years. I had a prophetic word given to me that spoke of me being an upside down cup, where I could not receive the water of God. But then there was a season of brokenness, and the cup was on its side. The Spirit of God was able to get into the cup a little, but was unable to fill it up. But praise God, the one prophesying saw that now my cup was upright, and I was receiving all God has for me. My cup was filled to overflowing, and began to flow everywhere around me. That is what the Lord has for you too. So praise Him. Worship Him. Raise your arms to Him and ready yourself to be filled to overflowing. It is the only way. Let's walk through some of the Psalms and praise Him together.

> Dear God, I lift my hands to You in Praise,
>
> Oh Lord, my Lord, Your name fills the earth! Your glory is higher than the heavens. I sing praises to Your name, O most High. Every good thing I have comes from You. Lord, You alone are my inheritance, my cup of blessing. You guard all that is mine. The land You have given me is a pleasant land. What a wonderful inheritance! I will not be shaken for You are right beside me. You show me the way of life, granting me the joy of Your presence and pleasure of living with You forever. I love You, Lord. You are my rock, fortress, redeemer and Saviour. In You I find protection; You are my shield and

Break Forth

the power that saves me. Lord, You are worthy of praise. You save me from my enemies. You light up my darkness. In Your strength I can crush an army and scale any wall. Your way is perfect. You have given me the victory. Your right hand supports me. You have made a wide path for my feet to keep them from slipping.

The heavens proclaim Your glory. The skies display Your craftsmanship. Your instructions are perfect, reviving the soul. Your decrees are trustworthy, making wise the simple.

Your commandments are right, bringing joy to the heart. I shout with joy because You give me victory. Your unfailing love keeps me from stumbling.

You, Lord, are strong and mighty, invincible in battle. O Lord, I give my life to You. I trust in You, my God! You are the God who saves me. All day long I put my hope in You. You are merciful, O Lord. You are good and You do what is right. You show the proper path to those who go astray. I worship You, Lord, in the splendor of Your holiness. Your voice is powerful and majestic. It splits the mighty cedars. I will exalt You. You brought me up from the grave. I sing to You, O LORD. I praise Your holy name. You have turned my mourning into dancing and clothed me with joy. I will not be silent. I will give You thanks forever! You bless me with peace, Oh mighty Father. Thank You, Lord.

(Adapted from Psalms 8, 9, 16, 18, 19, 21, 24, 25, 29, 30)

Break Forth

> The LORD hears his people when they call to him for help. He rescues them from all their troubles. The LORD is close to the brokenhearted; he rescues those whose spirits are crushed.
> *Psalm 34:17-18*

> To all who mourn in Israel, he will give a crown of beauty for ashes, joyous blessing instead of mourning, festive praise instead of despair. In their righteousness, they will be like great oaks that the LORD has planted for his own glory.
> *Isaiah 61:3*

> You have turned my mourning into joyful dancing. You have taken away my clothes of mourning and clothed me with joy, that I might sing praises to you and not be silent. O LORD my God, I will give you thanks forever!
> *Psalm 30:11-12*

Break Forth

> I waited patiently for the LORD to help me, and he turned to me and heard my cry. He lifted me out of the pit of despair, out of the mud and mire. He set my feet on solid ground and steadied me as I walked along. He has given me a new song to sing, a hymn of praise to our God. Many will see what he has done and be amazed. They will put their trust in the LORD.
> *Psalm 40:1-3*

> For he will conceal me there when troubles come; he will hide me in his sanctuary. He will place me out of reach on a high rock. Then I will hold my head high above my enemies who surround me. At his sanctuary I will offer sacrifices with shouts of joy, singing and praising the LORD with music.
> *Psalm 27:5-6*

Break Forth

Dear Child,

    My peace grows within you. Drink it in. Feel it wash over you. It will sustain you today. Walk in it. Walk with Me. I will sustain you. The truth will be revealed as you seek Me. Hold hard to My truths and you will see deliverance. My grace overwhelms you. Be overwhelmed by My grace. Do not grow weary. Be sustained by My power, My love as it flows out of you. Walk strong in the grace and truths I am giving you. You will walk in My power, not in your own strength. Rely on Me and I will carry you. Put your head up. Put your hands up, worship Me. Give Me your heart. I will put life back in it. Your heart grows lighter as you give your burdens to Me. My yoke is easy and light. The weariness comes from trying to do it on your own, from trying to figure it all out. Rest in Me, Child. I will carry you, lead you, guide you, whatever it takes. We are in this together. Rejoice in everything and you will find the joy you seek, My warrior daughter. Your heart grows thankful. In that I am well pleased.

    ♥ Jesus

Chapter Three

Healing from Addictions

You do not just have pain without a source. Pain is a symptom, not a disease. If I masked only the symptom, the actual "thing" ravaging my body would continue to flourish.

Calli J. Linwood

I WAS DESCRIBING MY FIGHT WITH HEADACHES WHEN I WROTE THAT. (See "Just Another Chapter.") But God gave me an understanding of that principle on a whole new level. Sometimes when we are seeking healing and lasting change in our lives, we spend all our time and energy trying to understand, control or stop the "symptoms." We falsely believe they are the problem, and if we rid ourselves of them, all would be well. However, by chasing the symptoms, the actual issue, which, in fact, causes the symptoms, is left with free reign to expand until it suffocates the healthy parts of our lives.

Symptoms can be such things as alcoholism, drug abuse, pornography, overeating, overspending, being too busy, anger, promiscuity, anorexia, gambling, speeding up, shutting down, cutting, creating chaos ... the list goes on. Symptoms are anything you do in attempt to not feel the pain that is constantly attacking your mind and heart. They are the things you do to try to prevent yourself from feeling anything as your world comes crashing down on you. But in the end they only increase your suffering, for though they temporarily numb the pain, they come steeped in guilt, shame and the destruction of your body, mind, finances, career, family, friends and faith.

Often, all the focus of healing is mistakenly put on trying to change these devastating habits that are seemingly destroying every facet of our lives. Family members might ask, "Why can't you just stop drinking?" We might tell ourselves "If only I could stop _____, then everything would be okay." (You fill in the blank.)

Coming through situations of abuse and trauma, there is much pain we want to forget; we desperately need to forget. So it is not truly shocking that many of us fall into some form of these addictions, some more destructive than others. But in order to receive healing, we need a shift in our thinking. Walk through this with me the way God revealed it: take one hand and clench it into a tight fist. This represents the wounds and the pain from living the life of the abused or traumatized. Now put the other hand over top of the clenched hand. This represents whatever coping mechanism we have chosen to dull the pain enough so we can just survive. Now, if the focus of healing is just on trying to pull off the top hand, we are still left with the clenched fist of pain ... and now it's worse because it is fully exposed. In order to survive, we

Break Forth

naturally just keep putting back the covering hand (returning to pain numbing behavior). Then we, or others around us, just keep trying to pull it off again, and again. In his teaching, *Seeing in the Spirit,* Graham Cooke[3] notes that what we focus on, we give power to. It's time we took the focus off the symptoms—the alcoholism, the overeating, etc., and direct our attention to healing the pain underneath—the pain that is causing us to need the covering. Think of it. You ___(drink)___ because you want to ease the pain. If the pain was gone, you would no longer need to __(drink)__, so therefore the __(alcoholism)__ would be gone too. (Adapt as needed.)

So no, you are not an alcoholic, a _____, or a _____. Stop declaring this over yourself. That is NOT who you are. That is NOT who God created you to be. You are God's masterpiece. You are the temple of the Holy Spirit. You are a child of the Most High God. You are no less than the daughter of royalty. Speak this truth over yourself. Yes, you may have a problem with _____ at this time. But this is not your identity. Know this. Believe this. Change your thinking. Do not give attention to the addiction. Focus on what you need to do to get healed, healthy, and whole. That, and Jesus should be the centre of your thoughts.

God loves you and wants to exchange every tear you've shed for His freedom, joy and peace. And He can do this. He will do this as you come before Him in honesty and in truth. Lay it all before Him on the altar. Give Him permission to walk you through the pain you will have to face for your healing. It will be hard for a season, but you can do this. You have already been through much harder things. You are a tough one. This I know.

My prayer team sees you as a diamond. Diamonds are formed under high pressure and hot temperatures. In itself, it just looks transparent—like nothing is there; there is nothing in it, and it has no use. But as the light shines through the diamond, it sparkles with every color of the rainbow and shines in every direction. As the light refracts and reflects off all the facets, the light shines in gorgeous beauty and vibrancy wherever He wants it to go. Even before God made the world, God loved you and chose you in Christ to be holy and without fault in His eyes (Ephesians 1:4). He made you as this diamond, and you are His. Let's pray.

> Dear God,
>
> Thank You, Father, that You have called me out of the darkness and into the light. Thank You, Lord, that it is You who breathes the breath of life into me, so even when I can't breathe on my own, when things around me are piling up so hard and fast I can barely breathe, You are there to do it for me. You will be the deep breath I need to sustain me. I ask You to remove any cloaks of guilt, shame, discouragement, fear, anxiety, anger, resentment, and bitterness that keep me holding my breath instead of breathing freely in a life of abundance. Thank You that You are holding me in the palm of Your hand, and telling me that You have me covered, so I can once again just breathe. I cast off any tactic of the enemy that tries to keep me or put me back into that place of barely breathing.
>
> I thank You, Father, for taking me through this tough, traumatic journey, and in it You have made me strong. I thank You for continuing to

strengthen me as I come to You in humility and honesty and lay every part of my life at Your feet. Please help me, because I cannot help myself. I give You all the parts of my life that are out of control, and I put them in Your control, Lord. I place myself in complete vulnerability as I lay before You every fear, every care ... everything I have tried to figure out on my own, and I allow You to do the work in me.

Help my feet to walk along the narrow path as You, the Lamp unto my feet, light the way. Show me what I need to do, Lord. Show me where I need to go, and keep me from wavering. You are the light in my darkness, Lord. You are the joy in my heaviness, and the lifter of my chin. In You I have no shame. Open my eyes to see, and my ears to hear, and set my heart to the beat of Your heart, so I can follow and catch the light You offer me. Thank You, Lord, for the high calling You have on my life, whether I can see it at this point or not. You know the original design in which You created me, so please help me to return to that original design, and to walk out the incredible destiny to which You have called me.

Lord Jesus, right now in Your name I break off every lie I have heard and every lie spoken to me or about me, or that I have spoken over myself. I declare that those lies will not hold me back any longer. I cut off every tormenting thought, sound, voice and word spoken against me, in Jesus' name. Lord, thank You that You are always here for me.

Break Forth

> Thank You that just like You are in the midst of the darkness while the butterfly struggles to free itself from the cocoon, so too, are You with me in my dark times of struggle. Through this journey, You will make me strong and resilient, and You are preparing me to fly with color and beauty. Help me to go where You ask me to go and do whatever You ask me to do. I thank You for making the changes in my life I need as I let go of all the things controlling me.

As a symbolic gesture, walk through this next section in the physical by miming the actions as you declare them in the spiritual. I believe by doing things in the natural, they allow a release in the spiritual.

> Lord, I put in my hands _____ (the addiction). I now raise my hands up to You, holding it before You. Take it from me. Take it from my life. I turn from it right now and ask for Your forgiveness. I thank You for the peace You are instilling in me as I let go. Thank You for setting me free … in Jesus' name. Amen

Break Forth

The prayer team prays a mother and father's blessing over you:

We pray that the love of the Lord surrounds you, that you know the love of the Father; that you feel His love. We pray you know deep within your heart that you were fearfully and wonderfully made and you do have a destiny and a purpose. We pray that you know you are worth more than you believe right now; you are worth more than you could ever imagine. You are a diamond in the rough and you are loved. We pray you may know that love. We pray the Father will turn your ear to wisdom and apply your heart to understanding. Despite all you've done, may you know there is forgiveness and hope and help. We pray you know Jesus died on the cross for you, and there is nothing you could have done that will change that. We pray God will bring people into your life to support you and help you see the truth. We pray God will help you move out of the lies and into the truth. The Lord is a good Father and He's there for you. We pray you come to understand this truth in a powerful way. We thank the Lord for who you are, especially right now. We pray in the name of Jesus Christ, Amen.

Break Forth

So now there is no condemnation for those who belong to Christ Jesus. And because you belong to Him, the power of the life-giving Spirit has freed you from the power of sin that leads to death.

Romans 8:1-2

So letting your sinful nature control your mind leads to death. But letting the Spirit control your mind leads to life and peace.

Romans 8:6

Yet now he has reconciled you to himself through the death of Christ in his physical body. As a result, he has brought you into his own presence, and you are holy and blameless as you stand before him without a single fault.

Colossians 1:22

Break Forth

Oh My Little One,

    Take heart. This is not the life I have for you. This is not the life I have designed for you. Come under My design, the true design of who I created you to be—the one who walks in freedom, in health and joy—the one who can't stop smiling at all the little things in life that make it amazing. My heart breaks over the losses you have suffered. But surrender them over to Me and I will mend your heart and dry your tears. Oh My Little One, the sun will shine again as you step into My light and My love. The rainy days are no more. Take My hand and I will guide you out of this haze that covers your life and hides that beautiful smile; the one I want the world to see.

♥ Jesus

Chapter Four

Drowning Out Bitter Roots

Chaos tends to be created in every aspect of co-parenting and finances in toxic relationships during a marriage, and especially after its dissolution. Everything that can be made difficult is made difficult—intentionally. Undermining and sabotage come at every turn. Early on, I remember excitedly staying up late to prepare for a Christmas cookie exchange, only to receive a phone call that dictated my plans had again been thwarted. He would not come home to be with our little kids. I could not go. Disappointment rolled in over me. (My mom ended up saving the day!) It would only get worse as the years progressed. I soon learned never to get my hopes up that things would turn out as I had planned or as I so desperately wanted.

Break Forth

I remember the embarrassment as the entire sports team sat waiting for me in the parking lot. I was frantically putting "Child Care Plan B" into action as Rob, mad at me again, was long gone, exacting his vengeance on me without a thought to all the others involved. I began to always expect the worst, as that seemed to always be what was.

During married life, Rob made sure I knew it was pointless to even look at the cute little tent trailer for sale at the neighbors' place. But soon after we went our somewhat separate ways, a favorite past time of his was camping in a friend's R.V., and eagerly taking the children to look for a camper of his own. Never having taken an actual holiday together in all our married years, then seeing Rob and the kids flying across the country or off the continent every year since ... I admit, felt like a knife in my back. Agreeing to pay equally for the kids' needs, then somehow most of the bills ending up on my side, and being blackmailed into going along with his financial decisions, have been constant roots of bitterness. Not picking up the kids at the agreed upon time, or even at all, sent me scrambling again and again. Unexpected phone calls forcing changes never discussed, and Rob's constant switching of the parenting schedule and making up new rules every time, continually sent me into a panic to rearrange once again, everything I had already so carefully rearranged. (Deep breath! Heavy sigh ...)

It seemed as if it was a never-ending merry-go-round that wasn't so merry. Always having to make plans and back up plans, then switching to plan C when he stepped in and disrupted everything I had rearranged because of his actions in the first place, was beginning to cause much stress and anxiety in my heart. (More heavy sighing.) I do thank God for my family and friends, who so understandingly would remain flexible and on-call at a moment's notice. They soon learned the depths of the disruptive nature of my co-parenting life.

Break Forth

Though I was no longer in the same kind of danger as when I lived in domestic violence, Rob used the tactic of intimidation for several years after. Pushing his way into my vehicle or blocking my exit from a room forced unwanted conversation. Intimacy was forced as well, with unwanted touching and coerced hugs in front of the kids. Inappropriate sexual comments and suggestions were made into my ear. And still, every few months I would endure a verbal assault that would leave me feeling shaken, unprotected and bare. I believed these things would never stop, never change, never be better; my life would always be characterized by these attacks.

My life was not peaceful. I lost hope that things would change, or be better at any level. I expected the worst and I got the worst. I had allowed all my unmet needs to lead to bitter root expectations. But soon, through my journaling time with God, He exposed the lies I had believed, and that I still allowed to govern my life. They were not the truth. What may be true in your life is not **the truth**. It does not set you free. The truth sets you free.

Through my experiences, I began to believe and expect that I wouldn't ever be loved, supported, healed, or have people in my life that helped me. I felt I wouldn't ever be healthy, whole or happy. I felt I was not allowed to have good things happen to me, and that the things I wanted or liked were wrong, or would eventually be taken away from me. If I liked or wanted something, I felt guilty or would be scared. I didn't want to get my hopes up, or dream again, because it wouldn't happen anyway, and if it did, it would be taken away from me. I believed if things were going well for too long, I had to start shutting it down and stop enjoying it. I had to instead start getting ready for it to be taken away from me. I always expected every good thing in my life to come tumbling down around me, because that is always what had happened in the past throughout the cycles of abuse.

Break Forth

I took on an attitude of "Why bother? I'll only be disappointed again." Disappointment, discouragement, despair and fear still controlled my life. As God was revealing these roots in me, He started speaking to me about how I needed to trust Him; that He will give and take away according to what is best for me as a whole, but not as a punishment, or because I didn't deserve good things, didn't expect good things, or even because that had been the pattern in my marriage. I was righteous in God's eyes because of the cross of Christ, so it was time to "expect the big things in God, the things I dismissed and discredited for myself" (prophetic word Aug, 2012) because of the condition of my heart. I had to remove the debris and clutter from my heart so I could experience God more. I had to ask God to help me yearn for Him more, and lessen my desire of other things; seeking the presence of God above all other things. I had to ask God to help me come to an understanding and belief that I could not have a holy desire or need that the Lord could not meet.

Bitter root expectations come from unmet needs. And yet, my God can meet all my needs. (Every want too, if my wants are in alignment with God, but that is another story!) This is the truth of His Word and His promises. I knew I needed prayer to catch this revelation and hold it in my heart as the truth. So, I went to two of my Spirit-filled friends who are well equipped to help people heal and hear God's voice in situations. I knew this was a root that grew incredibly deep in my heart, so I steeled myself against what I thought would be the tortuous pain of the knife in my chest digging out the root that had its tentacles wrapped around so many layers of my heart. Before they prayed, one of my friends felt she should sing the children's song over me, "He Poured in the Oil and the Wine." As they sang, something broke in me, and I wept. As I did, my other friend shrieked in delight, seeing in the spirit that the root was drowned with the oil and the wine, and floated out painlessly. It was a soft and gentle healing.

Break Forth

From there, I was able to surrender every need I felt was unmet, and every situation still tormenting me. I gave them all to God. My focus came off the needs, and on to the One who meets my needs. I gave Him the biggest source of chaos in my life—how Rob used the kids' schedule to its greatest potential of making things difficult for me on an almost daily basis. It's just like God that now, when Rob tries to sabotage my plans, they usually end up exceedingly better for me in the long run! I love when God does that!

At times I am still left in a bind, still left financially struggling, and still verbally assaulted, but these realities no longer have the same devastating impact on my soul. I am no longer the same person who only expected the worst in her life and for her life. Instead, I am expecting HUGE things in God. That is the opposite spirit of bitter root expectations—having great expectations of all the Lord has for me, and of all He plans to do in me and through me. You hold in your hands the very proof of that. I am incredibly honored and privileged that the Lord our God has called me to walk with you in your healing journey. It is truly above any and all expectations I could have imagined for my life. (And I even have a tent trailer now. True, it may be held together with duct tape—but it is all mine and I love it!)

And you, dear Reader, can also learn to have HUGE expectations in God. You are called to do your part (and He will help you with that) and He definitely will do His part. Put your hope and trust in Him alone, and allow Him to be your strong tower, your fortress, your everything. He will give you all you need. He will find so many creative and unique ways to encourage you as you learn to hear His voice clearly. He will teach you, step by step, as you put your hand in His for your journey. He will walk together with you on the inspired road you travel and light the way, right into the true destiny to which He has called you. Depend on Him and get excited about all He has for you ... some things for today, some for tomorrow, and some things waiting

Break Forth

just around the corner. He will put people in your path to encourage you and to help you as you ask. And remember, He is with you, and He will never leave you. Let's kneel together now and pray to wash out any roots of bitterness in your life, so you can expect the great and marvelous things God has in store for you!

> Lord, I thank You for everything You have taught me, and everything You have done for me, and continue to do for me. I ask now that You please give me the strength I need to put myself fully in Your hands for You to pull out any roots of bitterness residing in my heart, no matter how deep they run. I come against any desire of my flesh to self-protect, which would prevent my own healing. I allow You to take complete control of my healing, whatever it takes. I know it is my choice. I can choose to walk around with the pain of bitter roots in my life, which would be hard. Or, I can choose to surrender completely and do whatever it takes to get rid of it, trusting You to heal me. To do this I need to allow myself to be vulnerable and to face my fears, and this too is hard. But I trust You, Lord, that the freedom You will give me through it will be worth the price.

Break Forth

So, God, I pray You give me the great courage I need to be willing to lay aside my own control of the pain and how it is going to be dealt with and when it is going to be dealt with and how much it is going to hurt. Help me be willing. Stir up that desire. Stir up the willingness. Stir up the courage it is going to take to completely surrender that bitter root and trust You will remove it in its entirety.

Heavenly Father, You are the opposite of disappointment. I believe this won't be one more thing I am disappointed about; that I went through all this pain and again I am let down and left trying to do it on my own. I trust that as I lay myself bare before You, You will bring the healing of my heart I need. I pray I can embrace the healing You want to bring to me, Lord. Pour out the courage for me to be one hundred percent vulnerable, trusting You to completely do the work. Help me not shut down or pull away. Thank You that this healing is not begun in the flesh. It is begun in the Spirit and done by the Spirit and the flesh has no part in it. Help me be willing and eager to put myself solely into Your hands and under Your knife and trust Your surgical procedure, however You choose to pull out that root of bitterness.

Break Forth

I do pray You are soft and gentle with me. Reveal to me every single thing I am holding in my heart that is harboring bitterness; every situation, person, place, event—everything that has planted a root of bitterness in me. I pray You slowly and softly bring them to the surface and reveal them either one at a time or as a flood, but please reveal the key ones I need to present to You on the altar so I may be healed. Show me, Lord. (Give Holy Spirit time to reveal any situations that need to be presented to Him, then give them to the Lord as they are revealed to you.)

Lord, I give you _____. Please take this root as I lay it before You, and forgive me for holding on to it for so long. O Jesus, please help me to be able to forgive the people against whom I am holding bitterness. Do not hold them accountable on my behalf. I release them over to You to deal with. Please forgive _____ (names of people the Lord reveals to you that you need to forgive to release healing.)

Dear Lord, I pray against the lies that "It won't be worth it," "There won't be anything better," or "It is better this way or safer this way." I come against any self-protection mentality that says "I don't want to have any hopes because they'll just be thwarted again anyway." Help me to be willing to have hopes dashed and trust I'll still be okay, rather than being fearful of having hope and being stifled by self-protection.

Break Forth

I come against and break off fear and self-protection. I ask You to set me free from it in Jesus' name. I ask You, Lord, to reveal any other lies I have been believing. Show them to me please, Lord. (Allow time for any other lies to be revealed by Holy Spirit, and then break them off.)

Lord, I know there are trials in life; that things don't always go our way. Help me trust that in the big picture, You have everything under control and these trials are teaching me things and making me who You want me to be. All these work together in the plan You have for me, so my hope is in You.

Help me not be scared to hang on to You with both hands. Help me get up when I fall, and keep going when I am tired, so I can become who You are calling me to be while I am on this journey of healing. I know that when things don't happen the way I want them to or expect them to, the enemy can wreak havoc in my life and lie to me, saying, "Things don't work out for me," and "Things always go wrong." But Lord, teach me how to respond in a way that is pleasing to You, rather than reacting when things go wrong in my eyes. The enemy can't take that away from me, and that in itself is the victory.

I know it is not necessarily how things turn out in the end, but it is how I am handling it.

Break Forth

I don't have to go through these trials and tribulations furious, frustrated, anxious, depressed and such, but I can face trials with freedom, and a determination that I don't have to be bound and chained to past reactions and behaviors. Help me to rejoice over my new way of responding to those things. That is where the victory is. Help me understand that I can't control or change other people, make them change, or make them make sense. Help me realize I can't do anything about those kinds of things, but I can change the way I respond to them. I don't have to allow them to wreck my day, or life. That is gold. That peace is treasure from You, Lord.

So dear Lord Jesus, where these bitter roots are removed, I pray You come fill those places with Your Spirit so there would not be any emptiness, but only the fullness of the Spirit. Put excited expectations of all the things You are going to do in my life in those places. Let hope come like crocuses: when there is still snow on the ground, these little purple crocuses peek their heads through and exist in a hostile environment. They are pretty and delicate, yet they are hardy enough to poke their heads out through snowbanks. I am ready, Lord, to let that hope into my heart again. Do Your work in me. I trust You. In Jesus' name, I pray. Amen.

Break Forth

> Such things were written in the Scriptures long ago to teach us. And the Scriptures give us hope and encouragement as we wait patiently for God's promises to be fulfilled. I pray that God, the source of hope, will fill you completely with joy and peace because you trust in him. Then you will overflow with confident hope through the power of the Holy Spirit.
>
> *Romans 15:4,13*

> The high and lofty one who lives in eternity, the Holy One, says this: "I live in the high and holy place with those whose spirits are contrite and humble. I restore the crushed spirit of the humble and revive the courage of those with repentant hearts.
>
> *Isaiah 57:15*

Break Forth

Dear Child,

    I am here for you, by your side. Stay strong in My spirit. Do not be discouraged. Trust, hope, faith ... those are still your words. Those are still your heart. Be still your heart and receive those words. Receive all I have for you. Do not give up hope. My grace is sufficient. I will carry you through. Lay it all down before Me and I will pick it up and carry you. Your heart belongs to Me, so I will take care of it. Do not be overwhelmed with fear, but with My love and mercy and grace. I fill you with My peace. It flows all around you. Be filled by it. Drink it in. Place it all in My hands, Child. Do not be afraid. I will fill your heart to overflowing.

♥ Jesus

Chapter Five

Hidden Jealousy

Watching the family at Home Depot pick out stain for their deck, I cringed for my own loss. Knowing that in all likelihood, the dad will be the one heading up the project, or at least they will be doing it together, dropped that sadness in my belly as I hauled my purchase to the register by myself … and took it home by myself.

It takes me to the bittersweet memories in my head of when Rob and I too, were at Home Depot picking up the supplies to work on our yard. Working together on projects around our home was one thing at which we were successful. We could accomplish a lot of work in a short period, and do it really well. It was one area in which we mostly did not fight. These memories take my mind to that uncomprehending place of questioning why couldn't it have been like that for real, in all the other areas of our lives.

Break Forth

Other things too, bring up that sense of what I felt my life should have been like ... photos of unbroken families smiling in front of the Christmas tree, the Facebook images of these families on distant beaches, enjoying their yearly get-away ... seeing a little old man holding his wife's hand as he helps her get out of the car, still acting lovingly toward her after all these years. These images take me to that sad place of my heart of what never was, as our smiling faces in front of the brightly lit tree was most likely followed or preceded by some not-so-nice circumstances. And the arm around my shoulder at church was quick to disappear and the cold shoulder once again given as we retreated to the privacy of our vehicle. Those smiling-face-photos were never my reality.

So, being surrounded by the happy couples and families I see doing life together still brings up a certain amount of sadness in my heart that I do not have, nor really did have, an earthly husband who loved me. (Rob still faithfully reminds me of this fact, throwing in the ensuing sexual implication to ensure his sharp words have made their full impact.) I've always known this sadness was there, but I did not know how much destructive jealousy lurked beneath the sadness until I saw my own unattractive overreaction one afternoon. I had walked into a room in the middle of an ongoing conversation. Several ladies were semi-joking about their husband's inept misadventures when trying to get their kids fed and taken care of while "mom" was out of the house. I regretfully made a rather harsh comment that at least they had someone who tried to help them, so they shouldn't complain! I left the room, embarrassed by my sudden outburst, and discovered that along with the sadness, my heart was full of jealousy.

God showed me that my sadness brought with it the harmful jealousy that would attempt to destroy me if I didn't deal with it. Sadness and jealousy work together in tandem. The sadness makes me feel sorry for myself, which makes me feel unworthy, needy, ungrateful and unfulfilled. I then start to look at all the things I do not have, or may never have in life, and I get jealous of the people who I perceive have all I lack. I am then no longer satisfied with all the unique blessings, gifts and treasures God has specifically given to me. Once I start dwelling on these negative things, it puts despair and lack of hope into my head and heart. This lack of hope leads to lack of vision of what my life could still be like. And lack of vision ultimately brings death and destruction.

But God does not want this for me. He wants to fulfill my hopes, give me new dreams, and have me live a life that supersedes my expectations. When I find myself being drawn into a sad pity party, God allows me to go on a tangent in my journal, spouting off about all the things in my life that are difficult, unsatisfying, or sad. But He doesn't allow me to stay there. He then asks, "Now then, Calli, for what are you grateful?" A lengthy list emerges as I honestly consider all the positives. When I look at my life from this perspective, it changes things. No, I do not have some of the things others have, but I am immensely thankful for all I have been blessed with, and all that has been forged in my life because of my difficult path. Had I lived the fairy-tale life I once desired, I most likely would have neglected my relationship with the Lord. I would not have needed him so desperately, and probably would have unknowingly been satisfied with keeping Him on the outskirts of my life. Now I cannot imagine life without the intimacy with Him I experience.

So, I have two choices. I can choose to wallow in self-pity by focusing on the negative, which does not change anything and only succeeds in making me more miserable. Or, with the help and power of Holy Spirit, I can see life from God's perspective. I can be thankful in everything, and for everything, realizing that this is what puts me in the spiritual place I need to be. This way I can receive the abundant life God has promised me, as I remain obedient and faithful.

    I know sometimes it is hard to let things go, especially when they involve gross injustices committed against us with no remorse, and seemingly no consequences. But negativity breeds more negativity. It is time to get off the treadmill, and look at the scenery around us in a different light. There are times for venting to a close friend, or spouting off in your journal. God is big. He knows your heart anyway, so you can't fool Him in pretending all is well when you don't feel that in your heart. Share your heart with Him in truth and in all honesty. Share your hurts and your pain. Share your frustration. Share your anger. Share your jealousies and sadness. But don't stay there. Ask Him to help you see things differently. Ask Him to show you how to see things, and be open to His revelations, and your part in it. He'll do His part.

    I want to be that person in the grocery store that draws people to them with their infectious laugh and bright disposition. I do not choose to settle for being the gloomy soul that is perpetually bleak, downcast and sad. That is not the story God has for me. He wants joy to overflow in my life. He wants me to dance, rejoice and celebrate. Which story do you choose? Let's pray together, and lay down all that is causing you so much sorrow.

Break Forth

Father God,

Your Word says You are a jealous God. You are jealous for me, and that is a pure and holy thing. But Lord, the jealousy in me is that of the world, and it only causes strife. It breaks up relationships and wreaks havoc in my life and in the lives of others around me. I repent and renounce the spirit of jealousy. I don't need it. I don't want it and I will not partner with it any longer. Lord, please bring to the surface any specific areas of jealousy I need to bring before You so I can be free. Open my eyes so I can truly see it, and give me the courage to admit it and walk through it if I have been hiding it in any way; especially from myself. (Give time to Holy Spirit to bring specific things to your mind.)

Lord Jesus, I repent of _____. I turn that all over to You, Jesus. I do not want to carry it any longer. I ask You to forgive me and help me receive Your forgiveness. Help me see things differently—see them from Your perspective. Change my very mindsets and thought patterns.

Please reveal any lies I have been believing. If I have been believing my value and acceptance comes from man instead of God, I break that lie off, in Jesus' name. I ask You to instil the belief in my heart that I am worthwhile, valuable and more than good enough in Your eyes, because of the power of the cross.

Break Forth

Right now, I break off the spirit of jealousy in the name of Jesus, by the power of Holy Spirit. I break it off on my mother's side, right back to Adam and Eve, and on my father's side, right back to Adam and Eve. I break off the spirits of affliction and sorrow, in Jesus' name.

Lord God, please heal the broken relationships in my life caused by jealousy on my part, or on the part of others. Lord, please heal any ungodly responses or reactions I have to people because of any unhealthiness in this area. I pray for complete healing from all traumatic events caused by jealousy. I pray the blood of Christ to flow through and start healing the memories where jealousy took its toll.

Lord, wherever I am harboring anger or violence that has its root in jealousy, please help me speak it out and release it unto You. Do not let me look back on it, Lord. Strengthen me, Father God. Help me love myself as You love me, and see myself as You see me, giving me a new identity in Christ, which does not include any aspects of jealousy.

Lord, if there are any other areas where I have let jealousy control my life, or if I dwell on any material things or experiences others have that I do not, please reveal it to me and help me to surrender it unto You. The only thing I really need, Lord, is an intimate relationship with You. Father God, I know You are not the voice of condemnation, so You will gently show me the right way.

Break Forth

Shine Your light on my heart, God. I am ready.

Please restore joy to my life, Lord. Help me to be continually affirming and encouraging to others, and to be able to develop deep, intimate relationships with those you have placed in my life. Help me have trust and security in all my godly relationships. Bring a refreshing new start with a godly perspective to all of the people I am in contact with: my family, my friends, my colleagues, my communities, and even those who have hurt me or have shown jealousy toward me. Restore those relationships that even seem broken beyond repair. Please heal and seal any wounds in them and in me that were caused by unholy jealousy. Bring wholeness and health to all the people involved, in Jesus' precious name.

Fill up every part of my heart where jealousy was once rooted, with godly desires. Give me a heart with passion after You, and faith to believe that You will provide everything I need, and more, because You are truly a good God. Thank You, Father. I pray this in the holy name of Jesus.

Break Forth

Journal Entry - Spring, 2008

As hard as my life has been, I have been blessed with awesome, awesome, amazing family and friend—people in my life who reach out and go out of their way to touch my heart, my soul, my life, and let me know I am cared about, I am loved. I have experienced rejection at the deepest, most intimate level, leaving me bruised and vulnerable. Yet these people take a risk and I feel their hand on me, helping me through.

> So get rid of all evil behavior. Be done with all deceit, hypocrisy, jealousy, and all unkind speech. Like newborn babies, you must crave pure spiritual milk so that you will grow into a full experience of salvation. Cry out for this nourishment, now that you have had a taste of the LORD's kindness.
> *1 Peter 2:1-3*

Break Forth

Always be joyful. Never stop praying. Be thankful in all circumstances, for this is God's will for you who belong to Christ Jesus.

1 Thessalonians 5:16-18

You keep track of all my sorrows. You have collected all my tears in your bottle. You have recorded each one in your book.

Psalm 56:8

Those who are dominated by the sinful nature think about sinful things, but those who are controlled by the Holy Spirit think about things that please the Spirit. So letting your sinful nature control your mind leads to death. But letting the Spirit control your mind leads to life and peace.

Romans 8:5-6

Break Forth

Dear Child,

    My peace surrounds you. It floods over you. It washes out the sorrows, the pain, the frustration, the agony, the defeatist attitudes. Walk in confidence with your head held high, looking to the heavens, looking to Me, seeing Me in all of this. See Me in every step you take. I will be there. You're stepping out of the boat. You're trusting Me, so I will be there to guide you. I won't let you down. I won't let you falter. Feel My peace. See how it calms you. Treasure it. Let your whole being rest in My peace, the peace of a warrior. Feel it go deep inside of you. Revel in it. I am healing you. Rest in My presence while I do the work. I am healing you. I am restoring you. I am bringing you wholeness. I am touching those places of your heart that you have surrendered. I am healing you. Feel My touch. Feel My presence. It is deep. It is loving. Expect big things.

♥ Jesus

Chapter Six

Being Devoured

*The Lord took hold of me, and I was carried away by the
Spirit of the LORD to a valley filled with bones.
He led me all around among the bones that
covered the valley floor.
They were scattered everywhere across the
ground and were completely dried out.
Then he asked me, "Son of man, can these bones
become living people again?"
"O Sovereign LORD," I replied,
"you alone know the answer to that."
Ezekiel 37:1-3*

Break Forth

I HATE THE DEVOURING SPIRIT! IT EATS AWAY AT EVERYTHING IN AND around you! It robs you of your health, your vitality, your relationships, your time, your resources, your joy and your peace. It demands you operate in chaos and confusion. It torments and taunts you, keeping everything good and stable just out of your reach. It weakens your beliefs. It steals your morals. It stabs holes in the fabric of your identity. It causes mass destruction … and I could see it ruthlessly attacking my family.

An in-law family member and I were meeting with an amazing prayer warrior/counselor, who really understood the dynamics of spiritual warfare, to pray through some generational issues involving our families. The counselor was teaching us to piggy-back prayers off of scripture. (This means to read a verse and turn it into a prayer.) God interrupted the session by giving me a stunning vision of what the spiritual warfare occurring in our families looked like in the heavenly realm. The Lord showed me how it would destroy the future of the entire family if left to run rampant through the generations.

I saw a black army: soldiers dressed in black battle gear, heads and faces covered with full metal helmets, with only a rectangular slit where the eyes would be. They were carrying deadly weapons and riding black horses. There were so many in this army that I could not see any spaces between them, just soldier upon soldier, horse upon horse. As they rode across the sky, I saw this huge black blade descending from them and chopping up and down into our families. The heavy black blade kept going up and down, and I knew it was slicing up, tormenting, killing, destroying, devouring, massacring all the families of this generational line. Though I just saw the blade and did not see the actual destruction, I knew exactly what it was doing. And I knew it was an assignment against our family line, past, present and future.

Break Forth

We prayed against it, breaking it off under the authority of Christ, and we prayed protection for the family line. As we were praying, I saw the black army crumble into a grayish-white powder and fade away, much like smoke would fade and disappear, but much more quickly. I felt a heaving in my stomach that for me represents deep pain and anguish, and then I felt an excitement bubbling up. I had felt a great horror when the vision started, but an incredible victory by the end.

When God allowed me to see into the spiritual realm with that vision, it showed me how strong the demonic forces can be that come against our lives, and the destruction they can bring with them. But it also showed me how much more powerful the Lord is with His army, and how much authority we have with the cross of Christ. It was not even a battle. The black army coming against us crumbled immediately at the awesome power of the name of Jesus. Even though this spirit had been waging war against this family line for generations, it was dissolved as soon as it was recognized and called down in Jesus' name. The spirit was later named as the devouring spirit.

When I look back at my married life and the lives of past generations in this family line, I can see how much destruction was left in its wake. There is a hollow woundedness they carry, and a pervasive dysfunction in so many areas. I have seen firsthand the chaos this spirit demands. Things that could be so simply resolved with basic communication exploded into unforeseen disruptive forces. Everything that could go wrong in so many circumstances would go even worse, creating ripple effects that disrupted the lives of everyone around them.

So many times in life with Rob I saw this in action. The simple phone call that could have saved hours of worry, backtracking, planning, preparation, or rearranging things, was never made. I and any others involved were left waiting and wondering for hours on end as to what was happening, or to see if he would show up when he said he would, or even show up at all. Many times he refused to disclose his plans, even though it affected others. Or the opposite would occur—he would show up when he was not supposed to, and sabotage events, days or even entire weekends. This behavior was sometimes intentional, and sometimes just because the impending inconvenience simply did not affect him. Turning off his cell phone and forbidding the kids to answer the landline, or lying to them about who was calling, prevented me from putting rest to many situations. Necessary errands left undone, plans always left past the last minute, or changed after the fact no matter who was affected, constantly forced me into panic mode to make things right. Choices made based on spite and vengeance against me, formerly unfamiliar, became a disturbing part of my reality. So much of my time, patience, faith and sanity were all devoured.

My finances were eaten in our marriage as well. Un-agreed upon purchases were made—things to satiate his obsession with electronics and fancy items to create the right image for his business. Yet any extra money I received could only be used to cover our mounting debts. My desires and interests were deemed selfish, or not important. After all, I was just a teacher.

Time with my youngest child was also stolen through stubborn acts of defiance, as he refused to cooperate once the separation and divorce papers were signed. Demands to stay with a schedule specified by none other than Rob, forced my daughter into a daycare she hated on one of my two weekly workdays. Then on the many days I could stay home with my little girl by my side, he dragged her to his office, unwilling to let her stay with me if the schedule did not coincide. Flexibility and cooperation were not an option for him. Both precious time with my preschool daughter and my finances were again devoured unnecessarily, all in the name of his vow to not make things easy for me. Those weren't the only things devoured.

Break Forth

The enemy used Rob's harsh words, constant criticism and unsubstantiated belief that I was not good enough and nothing I ever did was up to his standard, to devour my very heart and soul. I was robbed of me; of the very person God had created me to be; the very person God loved, enjoyed, treasured and rejoiced over. As I dragged myself out of the relationship that day to safety, I look back in horror as I see what little was left of me—a mere remnant of my former self. My heart cries for that poor girl and all she had been through, and all she had lost of herself, of God, of life, of health, of hope … of all joy and peace. She had been ravaged in so many ways … physically, sexually, emotionally … her heart shattered so many times over. She believed she was broken beyond repair. She believed her soul would stay lost forever. How could she be restored after living for so long with the heavy foot of her oppressor on her neck? How could she once again stand tall and straight with her head up? How could her joy and peace be regained? How could she start to care and feel again? How could she start to be alive and love life again? How could all that had been devoured be restored?

I see those same skeletal remains in the women God now brings into my life. They are at the beginning stages of putting their lives back together; of putting their hearts back into their chests and asking them to start beating again—yet fearful of them doing that very thing. They see their journey ahead of them—that unscalable mountain range and those foreboding cliffs. They fear the road ahead of them holds nothing but the devastation with which they are so familiar. I look at them and my heart bleeds for them, and I cry out for them and I cry over them. Yet deep inside, my heart leaps for joy and my spirit stirs, because I know—I have experienced—the new life that only God can bring to those broken vessels. And I know God is waiting for them to only let go and take hold of Him with both hands, and He will more than restore all that was devoured. He will take the ashes of their burnt up

Break Forth

lives and breathe new life into them. He will not restore the old, but He will make them a new creation with a new song and a new dance; one that outshines the old in so many ways.

I have learned that being broken beyond repair is a marvelous thing because then God will make a new creation out of you. A friend gave me a prophetic picture from the Lord. In it, old, ugly, broken bricks were being taken from one pile and placed on the other side of the pile. The plain white surface of each brick was somehow transformed as each brick was carefully placed where it belonged, and it was creating a beautiful picture. What was once ugly, broken and despised, was now, at the hand of God, a beautiful picture that would draw others unto Him. That is my story. And that is why I am sharing it with you, for it is the story God wants for you too.

But the only way to come to this place of victory is to truly understand how to abide in the Lord. John 15:5 reads: "Yes, I am the vine; you are the branches. Those who remain in me and I in them will produce much fruit. For apart from me you can do nothing." But this concept is much like getting healthy physically. You can tell people that to do so they need to get plenty of rest and exercise, drink lots of water, eat healthy foods, and handle their stress properly. They promptly reply: "I have heard all that! Tell me something I don't know!" Yes, they have heard it, perhaps many times … but do they know what it actually means, and do they actually **do** it? The way the Lord taught me how to abide in Him was through a little pink plastic flower as described in the following story He gave me to write. He truly can teach us through anything!

Break Forth

Son Powered

The tiny spot of sun splashing into my classroom floor drew me to my knees in worship of the Father. My worship, cut short that morning, continued as I felt the rays shining strongly on my face. Peace flooded over me as I rocked slowly back and forth on my knees, soaking in His presence. Opening my eyes, I noticed the little solar-powered flower on the windowsill, gently swaying its head back and forth, and waving its tiny leaves softly up and down. Being drawn to it, I removed it from the sunlight. The movement soon faded and stopped. Placing it back in the sun, it resumed its peaceful swaying. Speaking to my heart, God showed me that we are much like that little flower. We need the Son to power us. We need to soak in His presence continually; basking in His radiant Glory constantly, becoming energized and empowered, or we too, will soon fade.

As the Lord was teaching me to abide in Him, He asked me to remove the distractions from my heart and mind and focus on Him. I had to believe He was all I needed, and to understand what that meant. I needed to stop worrying about the things of this world, and know He would protect me and provide for me in every area of my life, in His time. He asked me to turn my thoughts inward to the higher things of Him and focus just on spending time with Him. I could no longer allow myself to get so busy, even in doing things for Him, that I did not have time to spend with Him. He told me to

Break Forth

drink deeply in the morning by seeking Him, and as I spent more and more time in His presence, He would reveal things to me. And wow, He has!

He encouraged me not to give up, but that He would give me the strength when I felt overwhelmed at doing all the things I had to do just to keep up with life in general. Some days I felt I could not even do what I already needed to do, without adding anything else to my life. He gently urged me again not to let distraction and busyness rob me of all He had for me. If I did my part, He would do His part. I had to stay strong in carving out time for Him in my day. I was not to lose hold of all He had for me by being consumed with the little things of life; all the things on my *to-do* list that constantly called my name. He assured me they all would get done; that He would create time for me to accomplish all I needed to accomplish as I stayed true to Him.

My part was to stay focused on that voice that drew me to Him; the one that calls me to worship and dance before Him in trueness of heart. He whispered to my spirit that His time with me is precious; I was not to give it up; this was how He would work through me and with me. He promised to multiply my time as I trusted Him, and that He would put structures into place to help me; that He would keep carving out time for me as I did so for Him. Time is like money. The more you give to the Lord, the more you will seem to have. What seems impossible in the world is possible with Him.

And wow, wow, wow, wow! I have found this to be so true in my new life. Bits of time—a half hour of my lunch once or twice a week, and that half hour before bed when those home renovation shows formerly grabbed my attention—became precious time worshipping the Lord. I started a regular journaling time (See "Life Changing Words") in the mornings where I learned to listen to His voice instead of only pouring out my own. This session grew longer and longer as I hungered and thirsted more and

Break Forth

more after Him, and as He continued to be so faithful in feeding me, leading me, and touching the lives of others through what He would speak to them through me. I began to understand that spending time alone with Him is not an unnecessary luxury or an option, but is absolutely essential. I do not feel guilty, and no longer fall at the attacks of the enemy that scream at me that "I do not have time for this!" There are many occasions when I am right in the middle of things (such as the dishes), when a worship song calls me to drop to my knees and worship, or dance before the Lord. So I just do, and spend the time before Him until I feel released … and yet most days, those dishes still get done.

As I walk my journey now with the Lord, I finally truly understand what it means to abide in Him. He is our lifeblood and our source. He is the One that puts the breath back into our lungs so we can become fully alive again. It is through abiding in Him in spirit and in truth that we can rise up and be part of the army of the fully alive that He is calling.

Break Forth

My prayer team speaks this into your life:

Look into the face of Jesus, wounded one. His hand is stretched out towards you. He loves you. He'll touch you. He'll restore you. He will hold you in His arms. He will never leave your side. It is like you are a beautiful plant, but the weeds have come up all around you, trying to choke you, trying to keep the light from you so you suffocate. But the Lord is coming and digging all around you, and gathering up your roots, so He can bring you out of the weeds. He is bringing you to a place of glorious light where He will care for you so you may flourish, grow and prosper. You will, little flower, be able to lift your leaves and petals up to the Lord and worship Him—whole, happy and complete.

So, dear Reader, I ask you to put your hands over your heart. Now take your heart, and offer it up to the Lord. Ask Him to show you what abiding in Him means for you, and what it looks like in your life. Allow Him to make you into the new creation He desires you to be; perfect in His eyes. Come pray with us and let Him transform your life.

Break Forth

Dear Heavenly Father,

Thank You, Holy Spirit, that You are never far away from us. Thank You for Your love and compassion and for who You are. You hover over every hurting person, every broken heart. Thank You for hovering over me, and preparing the way for the Lord to speak. Thank You, Lord, that you separate the light from the darkness, and Your light shines over me with healing power to restore that which the enemy devoured. Thank You for bringing back life and health to my body, my soul, and my spirit to make me whole again.

Lord, thank You for taking my dead bones, sucked dry of all vitality, and causing them to vibrate with Your Spirit so they come alive again. Thank You for speaking life into my bones so they can be re-clothed with the flesh, the muscle and the skin that had been stripped from them. Lord, I pray You put Your breath into me, so I may come alive again. Lord, I pray new life and breath not only for me, but for the other dead, dry and weary ones. Let us all come alive again and stand up on our feet as the great army You are calling. Thank You that Your voice is power and life and only through You is this possible.

Lord, You are the God of restoration. As Jesus walked the earth looking into the eyes of the dying and embracing the sick, You made them whole again. You removed that which was eating away at them and replaced it with life.

Break Forth

Time and again You gave blind eyes sight, deaf ears could hear, and the lame walked. People were given back their dead from the grave. That is what You do, Lord. That is who You are. And that is what I am asking for; to be renewed and made whole in all areas of my life. I ask for light and vision for my life to be returned to me. (Ask Holy Spirit to reveal any specific areas of healing needed.) Lord, I specifically ask for healing in the area of _____.

Lord Jesus, by the power of Your name, I break off the devouring spirit from my life and send it to the foot of the cross of Jesus. I bind up this spirit in anyone in my life who is under its influence. (You can ask Holy Spirit if there is any particular situation needing to be addressed.)

Thank You, Lord, that You are delighted when we call upon Your name for restoration and healing. You delight in healing us and Your heart is always so rich and full towards the broken and wounded ones. It is only You who can heal us. Lord, thank You for opening the door to my healing. You open it and I just have to go through it, and you'll even help me to do that. Thank You that You are there on the other side of the door, smiling, beckoning me, ready to provide everything I need for my healing. I just need to allow my heart to receive it. Lord, I break off any fear that may try to hold me back from receiving all You have for me.

Break Forth

Lord, after being so hated and rejected, it is hard to understand how someone can love me as much as You do, and only want the best for me. But it is true. You loved me and chose me before the world began. You adore me and You adore everything about me. This perfect love is what heals and restores all that the enemy has devoured. How great is the love the Father lavishes on us, that we may be called the children of God. Please allow me to receive this truth and seal it way down deep in my heart. I love you, Lord.

Search for the LORD and for his strength;
continually seek him.
1 Chronicles 16:11

Stay alert! Watch out for your great enemy, the devil. He prowls around like a roaring lion, looking for someone to devour. Stand firm against him, and be strong in your faith.
1 Peter 5:8-9

Break Forth

Then he said to me, "Speak a prophetic message to these bones and say, 'Dry bones, listen to the word of the LORD! This is what the Sovereign LORD says: Look! I am going to put breath into you and make you live again! I will put flesh and muscles on you and cover you with skin. I will put breath into you, and you will come to life. Then you will know that I am the LORD.'" So I spoke this message, just as he told me. Suddenly as I spoke, there was a rattling noise all across the valley. The bones of each body came together and attached themselves as complete skeletons. Then as I watched, muscles and flesh formed over the bones. Then skin formed to cover their bodies, but they still had no breath in them. Then he said to me, "Speak a prophetic message to the winds, son of man. Speak a prophetic message and say, 'This is what the Sovereign LORD says: Come, O breath, from the four winds! Breathe into these dead bodies so they may live again.'" So I spoke the message as he commanded me, and breath came into their bodies. They all came to life and stood up on their feet —a great army.

Ezekiel 37:4-10

Break Forth

> The thief's purpose is to steal
> and kill and destroy.
> My purpose is to give them a rich
> and satisfying life.
> *John 10:10*

Prophetic word – December 2009

I don't want to put anything back together. I want to do something new. Trust Me. I am going to make something new. I am not just going to patch the old. I am going to make something new for you.

Break Forth

Dear Child,

    The enemy shall no longer rob, kill and destroy. He is no longer allowed to set foot in your camp. He cannot remain in the presence of a warrior. You are drawing on My power now. The enemy must flee. You are walking in the light. My light shines out of you. My love pours forth out of you. Feel My love. Feel My peace. Feel My presence. It will continue to pour out of you as you continue to walk with Me. Love, hope, trust – those are still your heart's cry. Your heart's cry is also for Me, and in that I am well pleased. Go forth, as My light and presence go with you. Shine for all to see. Let My Glory be known. Share My light, share My love. Let others dwell in My presence.

♥ Jesus

Chapter Seven

The Letters on My Forehead

I STARTED SLEEPING WITH A BASEBALL BAT UNDER MY BED WHEN THE voice on the phone switched from just talking about my anatomy, to threatening to come to my house. The series of obscene calls led to the police tracking down the culprit, and charges being laid. It turned out to be a shy and quiet former student of mine. His hormones had kicked in, and I was probably one of the few "girls" that had paid any attention to him. It was comforting to realize he wasn't some scary lunatic off the street, but the event did sharpen that edge of fear in my life, that once again, someone I knew had turned on me. It wasn't the first time, and it definitely was not the last.

Break Forth

The first time I saw Leo, he looked lost and lonely. I think that was what drew me to him. Out for a bike ride, I came across him playing alone in the street. By his demeanor and the conversation that followed, I thought he was maybe twelve years old. Later I would discover he was sixteen; the same age as I was. It was his eyes that told me, however, that he was different. They were beautiful but somehow vacant. Walking me all the way home, he seemingly was unable to let go. Soon, he began showing up on my doorstep, and my family and I, always having a heart for the lost ones, took him in under our wing. Supper at McDonalds and trips to church with us became the norm. Within the parameters of the relationship that had been established, I had thought nothing of bringing him with me to the movie theater with my friend and I that afternoon. I could not have been more wrong. With my friend inside the theater, he grabbed me and threw me up against the wall in the hallway, hissing, "Why did you have to bring her? She is ruining it." Roughly pinning me against the wall, he started talking about how we were going to get married. Heart pounding, dazed by confusion and scared, I broke free and ran.

That was the first of my assaults by someone known to me. I believe it was what opened the door to allow such violence in my life. Odd things became a part of my sixteen-year-old repertoire. I had to park a block away from my house and sneak through the neighbor's yard to get home as Leo sat for hours on end fixing his bike nearby. I had to hide away at my sister's house for a time, trying to evade my stalker. A knife in the yard and a flower in my windshield were clues to a suspicious break-in next door, and only amplified my fear. As I look back over that time period, I see the pattern of a victim mentality already being established: the fear, the shock and disbelief as your world begins to feel like a TV soap opera, the broken trust from someone you thought you knew, the hiding away to try to feel safe, always on the

Break Forth

lookout for someone to find you, to get you, to hurt you. This was such a foreshadowing to what became my life. I believe that was when the "V" for "victim" was branded on my forehead, and I adopted this mentality.

Another letter appeared on my forehead four years ago. It was a "D." And it was big and red and ugly. I did not like this letter any better than I liked the last one. In fact, I despised it. And I felt despised because of it. I felt ashamed and I believed I had lost the rest of the little dignity I had left. I felt this "D" robbed me of any respect from people in the church and in my school. I felt it left me unqualified for ministry positions. And I definitely felt it limited my relationships because I believed others saw me as a threat to the sanctity of the family. I was DIVORCED, and therefore I was not a good role model to anyone. I felt wives would think I was after their husbands, and husbands would think I was a bad influence … "one of those bitter divorced women" they didn't want their wives to be around.

Some people may have felt this way, but in actuality, there was no evidence to substantiate what I was feeling. But I do know that was my perspective. And it hurt. It changed the way I saw myself. But I know now it was only my perspective because of the letters I carried around on my forehead, which made their way into my brain and overtook my thinking. They formulated a perceived reality in my life that was not really there. They were lies of the enemy that I incorporated as part of my faulty belief system and were therefore permitted to influence my thought patterns, my behaviors and actions, and my whole emotional world. Worse yet, I allowed them to form part of my identity.

But I am so grateful that this chapter does not end here. **Who we are has nothing to do with what we have done, or what has been done to us. It is what has been done *for* us that makes us who we are.** The "Victim" label, the "Divorced" label, or whatever other label you choose to put on

Break Forth

yourself or others try to mark you with, has no impact on us when we learn who we really are. Our identity in Christ supersedes all labels, all marks. We are marked with the seal of the King. We are marked by the blood of the Lamb, and it covers all. The scriptures go into great detail describing who we are in Christ. (See "Overcoming Rejection" in *Walking Tall*.) But the fundamental truth behind all of it is that we are the beloved of God. The Lord of Heaven's Armies, the Creator of the universe, knows you—the real you—strengths, weaknesses, faults, scars and all, and loves you. You are adored, cared for, cherished and treasured. You are near and dear to the Father's heart. You are highly favored, highly regarded and highly valued. You are pleasing to Him, and oh so precious. You are the daughter of the King and the bride of Christ. You are the beloved. And it is time for you to speak it out loud, confess it and proclaim it:

I am the beloved of God. The Lord of Heaven's Armies, the Creator of the universe, knows me—the real me—strengths, weaknesses, faults, scars and all, and loves me. I am adored, cared for, cherished and treasured. I am near and dear to the Father's heart. I am highly favored, highly regarded and highly valued. I am pleasing to Him, and oh so precious. I am the daughter of the King, and the bride of Christ. I am the beloved.

Break Forth

Come, step out of the posture of the defeated and hopeless. Rise up and take your King's hand. Look full into His face and receive all He has for you. He's asking you to come. The courage to do this will be given as you ask.

Dear Lord,

    The victim mentality has pasted a "V" on my forehead, and it has brought with it so many other labels that I have been wearing. Lord, this goes deeper into my soul than I realize, and it has negatively impacted so many areas of my life. I need Your help! I know there is a brutal war being waged all around me, ensnaring me, keeping me gagged and bound, and away from all the treasures You have for me. It feels as if so many things in my life have been set up to be against me, time and time again.

    But Lord, I am ready to let go of the victim mentality and all its companions that have tried to conceal and steal my true identity and destiny. I repent for partnering with these spirits. I break them off of my life now in Jesus' name, right back to Adam and Eve on my father's side and on my mother's side. I will partner with them no longer, by the power of the cross. I renounce any pride that has kept me walking in this mentality, known or unknown.

Break Forth

I break off specifically the victim spirit, in Jesus' name. I break off any spirits of religion and legalism that are keeping any resources out of my hands and the hands of all other women in my situation. I stand, believing the time is now to break this off His bride! I stand in the fire right now for the release of the chains from me and from the other daughters of Christ that have been so trapped by the enemy. I remove every cloak of oppression from the enemy and the misuse of people in my life that try to reconfirm this victim mentality time and time again. I break off the predator spirit, in Jesus' name, and I place the cross of Christ between this spirit and myself and say "No!" to any more of its destructive forces.

Heavenly Father, hear your daughter's cry! The enemy wages war against me and Your other daughters, trying to silence us, to oppress us and to prevent us from doing what You have called us to do! I break off the spiritual forces that are attacking! Lord, break the chains of the enemy. Show me the strategy I need to come against this principality!

I put a guard over my heart and mind; a guard of Your blood, keeping me protected. Lord, bring freedom and release. Enemy, be silenced in Jesus' name, by His great authority.

Break Forth

Devouring spirit, I command you to go in Jesus' name. Stand down all powers and principalities and submit to the power and authority of Jesus! You will not have nor stop this daughter of the King! I have victory over you on all fronts!

    Lord, teach me how to not walk in the mindset of the victim. I repent of and break off any self-pity. Lord, I ask You to reveal to me now any other lies from the enemy I have been believing that has helped perpetuate this mentality. (Give the Holy Spirit time to reveal any other lies.) Lord, I break off the lie that Your promises are for everyone else but me, and the lie that _____.

I know, Lord, that the things that have happened to me were not my fault. I am not responsible for them, nor did I cause them to happen.

    I will keep my head down no longer. I choose to walk in the honor You have bestowed upon me, with my head held high, as fitting for the princess I am. I choose to not settle for any less than the perfect plan You have for my life, and for all the provision and bountiful blessings You have reserved for Your children. I choose to walk in joy and peace, as Your daughter. I choose to let my mouth speak words of trust, faith, fire and passion, rather than despair, hopelessness and defeat.

Break Forth

Rather than being helpless, I choose to rise up into the warrior You are calling me to be. I will rise up and fight to take the ground You have set before me, and I will not back down! I have all the authority of the daughter of Christ and I choose that in which to walk.

Lord, I love You. Thank You for loving me. Thank You for teaching me to be a warrior, and how to walk in God-confidence and strength. Thank You for healing me. I ask You to seal the work done in me at this time, and continue to reveal any areas that need healing. In all the places that the barbs of the enemy have been removed, please fill them up with Your peace and joy. Let me receive Your love deep into my heart, to never be removed. I pray all of this in the mighty name of Jesus Christ. Amen.

> My child, pay attention to what I say.
> Listen carefully to my words.
> Don't lose sight of them.
> Let them penetrate deep into your heart,
> for they bring life to those who find them,
> and healing to their whole body.
> Guard your heart above all else,
> for it determines the course of your life.
> *Proverbs 4:20-23*

Break Forth

Copy this verse where you will see it often and say it out loud daily, until it becomes written on your heart. As you speak and believe in your heart, so shall you be. (Proverbs 23:7).

> I am the beloved of God. The Lord of Heaven's Armies, the Creator of the universe, knows me—the real me—strengths, weaknesses, faults, scars and all, and loves me. I am adored, cared for, cherished and treasured. I am near and dear to the Father's heart. I am highly favored, highly regarded and highly valued. I am pleasing to Him, and oh so precious. I am the daughter of the King, and the bride of Christ. I am the beloved.

Break Forth

Child,

    Remember who you are. You are loved by Me, first and foremost. That is your identity. There is none other. You are wholly loved by Me. I know your heart. I know it all. You are a treasure to me in every capacity; the parts of yourself that you love and those you don't. You are created for a purpose; My purpose. I go before you and lead the way. Lay them down before Me. I will take you through the minefield that lies before you. Do not worry. I will navigate all the tricky steps. You are just along for the ride. You focus on your heart being right before Me and I will do the rest. Pray for those I put on your heart. Love on those who need it. Be gentle in word. Take the steps I put in front of you. That is your part. You will know. You will know. I will not let you fall. I will not let you fall.

♥ Jesus

Chapter Eight

The Shroud of Death

"Do you want to die? Do you ever want to see your kids again?" It was this threat—the threat to harm my kids by taking away their mom—that absolutely shook me awake and into my reality. In my head at the time, this was the first death threat Rob had ever made against me. But later, when my sister challenged me on this belief, I began to understand there were many of them.

Throwing me off a balcony, burying me under a golf-green, smashing my head with a remote control or through a windshield—all had the potential of ending my life had they been acted upon. I had no way of knowing if he was just trying to control me with fear, or if he was actually capable of any of it—intentionally or just in trying to teach me a lesson that perhaps would go horribly wrong. Either way, it resulted in the spirit of death and destruction entering my life.

Break Forth

I was not innocent in allowing it in my life either. There were times before I had kids that I entertained the thought that it would be so easy to end all my suffering ... one quick turn of the wheel while driving, either into a semi or off an embankment. Now I recognize those thoughts as a spiritual attack. For though I never considered myself suicidal, even my quick analysis of those thoughts before their dismissal was an open door in my life to the enemy. It was me partnering with death and destruction, no matter how brief.

When I whispered to my heart "I can't do this anymore, I can't live like this ..." without doing anything about it either to strengthen myself in God, or to change my circumstances, a little piece of me would die. My thoughts of *This will never change ... I'll never be okay ... Why bother to try anymore, it always just makes it worse ... No one can help me ... Is it worth it anymore? ... What is the point of anything anymore?* ... all stemmed from the assignment of death. I no longer had vision for my life, but was simply going through the motions; doing what I had to do to survive. Hope would flicker from time to time, keeping me going, but most of my dreams had died along with my joy. Even doing things I loved and the things that I was good at—all those things that had at one time brought fulfillment to my life—were always tempered with trepidation that somehow it would be turned against me, or it would eventually blow up in my face. I could not even fully enjoy watching my kids grow and thrive, as I was so fearful of their future. I was in no way living life but was instead trudging through, slowly dying.

God has shown me that everything preventing us from living life in the fullness of Christ—always advancing, always growing and building—and anything turning us away from the Lord, are subtle forms of death. I was indeed entrenched way over my head on this path. When I think back to the times of hands on my throat threatening to choke the life out of me, I shudder.

Break Forth

But it was constantly walking in the shroud of death that was my life that had a deeper, more devastating impact on my being.

Walking in discouragement instead of faith, defeat instead of victory, despair instead of confident hope, and depression instead of joy, was destroying the life God had intended for me. It was living under the spirit of death and destruction. Living life in a house of cards, all ready to come down, in a warped reality of deceitful promises and vengeance instead of love, was not my calling, nor my place. Nor is it your calling, nor your place. I learned through Cleansing Stream Ministries that confusion, selfishness, mistrust, suspicion, betrayal and broken trust are all part of this spirit. Relationships are dismantled. Mental capacities and emotional soundness are killed. Physical health is compromised or damaged. This is all according to the spirit of death and destruction.

But God wants to bring new life to us—resurrected life; the life that comes from the death of Jesus and the finished work of the cross. He wants to make us a new creation. We have victory through Christ, who loves us. We need to let go of all we are striving for, and all that is trying to smother us, and allow the Lord to guide us in His time. Each day you spend with Him gives you a little more life. You grow a little stronger. You grow a little closer to His heart, and you hear His voice a little louder. Each day you give Him encourages that confident hope He has placed within you to take root, and new visions for life the way He has designed, will be birthed.

As weak as you may be, grasp hard unto Him, and strength will come. He will open doors as you are obedient and continue to walk through them, fully trusting what He has placed on the other side. You will enter into new opportunities for healing and growth—ones you could not have possibly orchestrated for yourself; miraculous things that will leave you in awe of Him. Excitement will grow in your heart, and you will feel the resurrection

Break Forth

life flowing out of you—the life that is rightfully yours; not the façade of previous days.

As Jesus gets hold of your heart and life, and you continue to surrender every detail to Him, then He will take care of everything—all of it. I have learned that things are a lot more rocky and rough when I try to contain, control and calculate every aspect of my life. It is a scary process, putting everything in God's hands … kind of like jumping off of a cliff blindfolded. But as He scoops you up out of the air each time, and puts you softly down in a way you could not even invent, it gets easier. (And most of it is amazingly fun!) As you give your heart to the Lord and no other, prioritized as number one, He blesses you bountifully in matters of the heart, in time, in finances, in health and in relationships.

Your life will be so far from the wounded road you once walked, you will not even recognize it. They say hindsight is 20/20 … so though you may not have it yet, I do. That is why the Lord has asked me to walk with you. Let us pray so you can step into the new, resurrected life God has waiting for you.

Break Forth

Dear Heavenly Father,

Thank You that nothing can separate us from Your love and that in Your love for us, You gave us life in our body, soul and spirit—eternal life, to overcome death in every circumstance. Lord, I am not walking in the freedom that comes with that life. Many things distract and take me away from where You want me to be and who You want me to be. I've believed lies of the enemy that have brought a spirit of death and destruction upon me. Father, I repent.

I've believed such lies as "You're not enough, You don't deserve to live," and "You don't deserve good in your life." (Ask Holy Spirit to identify lies that have been whispered by the enemy). I break these off of my life now in Jesus' name. I will partner with them no longer. Thank You, Holy Spirit, for showing me that these are not from me, nor from the Father, but I am being accused by the enemy of my soul. I refuse to believe these lies any more. The power of deception over my life is broken, in Jesus' name.

Lord, I sometimes struggle with negative and destructive thoughts about myself and about others, which discourage me from being in a relationship with You and with Your people. Holy Spirit, give me a revelation and expose those thought patterns that are causing self-deprecating beliefs and trying to force me into isolation.

Break Forth

In Jesus' name I cancel beliefs that I am better off alone, or that others would be better off without me. I know You've created me for relationship. You are love and You are relationship. It is who You are, and it is one of the purposes for which I was created—to be in relationship with You and with Your people.

I repent of the times I have isolated myself as I fell victim to these lies, either physically or emotionally, instead of seeking You and others in honesty and truth. It has put me in a place of vulnerability where the spirits of death, destruction, suicide and the like could find an open door in my life. I choose to close that door now, in Jesus' name. Father, I break off any entrance points for these spirits generationally on my mother's and father's sides right back to Adam and Eve. Heal any trauma of my body, soul and spirit I have suffered, and remove any curse words spoken over me that have allowed these spirits to reign over me.

I silence the voice of the mocking spirit that taunts me, saying that nothing will help or change. I cancel its assignment over me, isolate it and cut off its authority, in Jesus' name.

I revoke all vows I have made in times of pain or despair that have caused me to partner with destruction in any form, allowing my body to start on the path to death. I speak life back into my body, soul and spirit. (Ask Holy Spirit to reveal any vows you've made).

Break Forth

And now I isolate that spirit of death and destruction. You have no power or authority in my life. I break off generationally all ties that you have on my mother's and father's sides right now. You have no permission or legal right to be here so I command you to leave, with all your lies and deception, in Jesus' name. Holy Spirit, I ask You to come and fill my mind, body and spirit. I thank You that You bring life, hope and joy. Thank You that You have a destiny and purpose for my life, that You want to restore my fortune, end my captivity and bring me home.

Thank You, Lord, that You desire for me to be in relationship, to love, to laugh and enjoy my life. I choose to receive this; I choose to walk in this. I choose to receive the spirit of life and the gifts God has for me. I am enough in Jesus. Thank You for loving me just as I am, and for loving me so much that You don't want to leave me where I'm at, but You want to give me abundant life. Your plans for me far exceed that which I could ever dream up on my own, and for that I am grateful. Lord, I want the future You have for me. I want the family, the relationships, the ministry and the freedom You have for me. I choose to walk in the full freedom of salvation.

Thank You, Father God, that Your grace and mercy extends far beyond what I deserve. Help me to serve others, bless others and encourage others. Help me to serve You with all my heart. Help me to walk in everything to which You are calling

Break Forth

me. I pray for a new level of joy to be released in my life as You touch me. Bring the shift about in my spirit that takes me from doubt and despair to full confidence in being able to walk in the calling for which You have designed me. Thank You for strengthening me. Thank You for who You are in my life and for loving me as much as You do. I pray this in Jesus' name. Amen.

> But the LORD watches over those who fear him, those who rely on his unfailing love. He rescues them from death and keeps them alive in time of famine.
> *Psalm 33:18-19*

> In his kindness God called you to share in his eternal glory by means of Christ Jesus. So after you have suffered a little while, he will restore, support, and strengthen you, and he will place you on a firm foundation. All power to him forever! Amen!
> *1 Peter 5:10-11*

Break Forth

> For you have rescued me from death;
> you have kept my feet from slipping.
> So now I can walk in your presence, O God,
> in your life-giving light.
> *Psalm 56:13*

Dear Child,

    Do not let go. I will pull you up, but you must not let go. I will take you out of the depths of despair that hold you down; that threaten to snuff the life out of you. I will be your rear guard. I will protect you. You are the treasure of my heart. Your life is so very precious to me, My child. It stirs affection deep in My heart that is unmatched in all of creation. My desire to see you live fully free is also unmatched. I will bring you into that place if you let Me. I will bring you out of those deep waters that threaten to drown you. Turn your heart to Me and I will set you on the path that leads to freedom. Trust, My child. That is the gateway that leads to all I have for you. The table is set and the invitation is made. What do you say, Child, what do you say?

                                                           ♥Jesus

Chapter Nine

Unheard Apology

*A*BUSE... NASTY STUFF. IT IS ONE OF THOSE THINGS THAT YOU TRULY don't understand the depths of its destruction until you have walked in it. Don't say, "It wasn't that bad." You only feel this way if you know no other way anymore. Like a frog in boiling water, you get used to the turmoil; forgetting it will eventually take its deathly toll. Don't say, "It was really my fault, I pushed him." No matter what you did, no matter what you said, it did not warrant the exaggerated violent response nor the awful words that forced their way into your soul, coloring it black.

It is not right what happened to you. It is not just. It is not fair. You bore the brunt of another's shame, of another's pain, of another's anger as he lashed back at the world. You were caught in the crossfire of a fight not your own. You were bruised, either on the surface or deep in your heart; it makes no difference which. Both inflict the same kind of wound. You ache for some

Break Forth

acknowledgment that what happened to you was not right, not just, not fair. But you never hear the words. Or, you have learned not to trust them, for they are just another sandcastle on the beach, anyway.

But I know what happened to you is not right, not just, not fair. **It is not right. It is not just. It is not fair.** And so on behalf of this person who did this to you, I am truly and deeply sorry. I am sorry for your hurt. I am sorry for your pain. I am sorry for everything your poor heart had to carry for all this time. I am sorry for each day you had to struggle through, feeling like you were going to break. I am truly sorry that in all the places and circumstances where you should have received love, joy, affection and honor, you instead were stripped bare; robbed of all that should have been given to you. I am sorry I did not stop what was being done to you. I am sorry I did not listen; that I left you as one of the voiceless ones. I am sorry I did not help you. I am truly, deeply sorry.

Now I ask for your forgiveness, so your heart can be set free. You deserve that. You deserve to move forward in life with pure joy that comes from a heart fully healed. And your heart can be healed; if only you open it enough to let the pain out and let God's grace come in. Be brave. You can do this. You have been through much worse. You are a tough one. This I know.

♥ Calli J. Linwood

Part Two

Spiritual Development

Walking with God is like any other skill you learn. It is hard at first—unfamiliar. You are not quite sure how to go about it, or what to expect. It seems foreign and ill-fitting. But as you practice and grow in it, and spend more and more time, it becomes familiar; easy—as if your body, soul and spirit just know how to do it. As a baby goes from holding up its head, to rolling over, to crawling, walking, and running, so too is it with your spiritual development—awkward and slow at first, to more and more proficient, until you are galloping and leaping. Then God gives you more and more, faster and faster ... until you know this skill so intimately that soon ... you are flying ...

Chapter Ten

Do My Prayers Matter?

The atmosphere in the gym had turned nasty surprisingly quickly. It wasn't even the second half of the game yet. Though his team was winning, the opposing coach was yelling profusely at his players, and his physical demeanor was more than unpleasant. As I sat on the bench as the trainer of the high school girls' basketball team, I was thinking that this game was already out of control, and was only going to get more so as it progressed and tensions mounted. This leads to people's conduct becoming irrational—it is then that people get hurt, emotionally and physically. I was actually quite alarmed about the situation, but I had no control over any aspects of the game. I could only pray, as the atmosphere in the gym grew more tempestuous.

Break Forth

I started to pray continuously in the Spirit. Within the next hour, our team was winning, and given the other coach's previous words and attitude, he, in all earthly reasoning, should have been absolutely furious by then—but he wasn't. He was totally calm and rational. The entire atmosphere in the gym had shifted. The storm had passed, and the ugliness was gone. We won that day, but my prayers had not been about that at all. I do not know if anyone else was praying that day, but through it, God showed me how prayer can change the entire atmosphere. At that time, however, I did not believe my prayers had brought about any significant spiritual shifts. My doubts and unbelief got the better of me, and it wasn't until a similar event months later, and God reminding me of the two, that I fully understood that yes, my prayers do matter!

The second experience started with God giving me a specific prayer assignment. My reaction was, *If praying over all the chairs and the speaker before chapel is so important, why isn't someone more spiritual than I doing it?*

What was God's response? *I didn't ask them, I asked you!* So what could I do, but pray? Opening my eyes a time later to see the chapel speaker slumped over the back of a chair was a shock, indeed! I tentatively tested the thought that maybe he was heavy under the weight of Holy Spirit ... after all, I had been intensely praying for him. But even after his passionate message with tears in his delivery, I convinced myself that my prayers had no impact. After all, I was only one small, insignificant person.

But it would all be put to rest in my spirit when the Lord reminded me of these times in tandem, and told me that He had, in fact, answered my prayers in both incidents. At that, all the heavy prayers for others from times past came flooding to the forefront of my memory ... of a baby born to an infertile woman, breakthroughs in finances, new life in broken relationships.

Break Forth

Whether I was just one of many saints presenting the petition before the Lord, or if I was just one, my prayers did matter, and they do matter. So do yours.

God says to bring everything to Him in prayer. Sometimes we get discouraged because we don't see the answer to prayer we want, or we were expecting. Or the answers don't come fast enough for our liking. But God has shown me that sometimes our desired result does not fit at all into His bigger plan, and perhaps would even be detrimental to us, or to those around us. As well, His timing is perfect, and therefore much wiser than our own! We have to learn how to have complete trust in this and in Him. Tragedies happen. People we pray for, die. Circumstances present the worst-case scenarios. I don't even pretend to know why this is the way it is, I just know I need to pray for everything God shows me, until He releases me from it. And then I just have to trust that His will is done.

As you spend more time in His presence, you get to know the Father's heart better and better. This alignment of your life to His Spirit helps you walk in the center of His will for you, and thus your prayers begin to align more and more with His Father's heart. That is what gives them the power and authority He desires to give them. As you begin to understand how He operates in and through your life, you come to recognize the specific prayer assignments He gives you. When the King of all creation gives you the honor of partnering with Him to transform lives, set captives free and bring about profound changes—you take that seriously. But fear not, He will show you how. He will give you the strategies you need in more and more detail as you learn to discern His voice. Then you have to trust that His will is done. This obedience is one aspect of our part in prayer.

Another aspect of our role in prayer is to pray for ourselves as King David did; crying out to God for Him to pull us in so tightly to Himself that we cannot help but to know the heart of God. And then this will be reflected

Break Forth

in our prayers. Every day, as you spend time with Him and pray for others, do not neglect praying for yourself. As you do, God will strengthen you, purify you, give you knowledge and wisdom, encourage you, pour out His love, mercy and grace on you, and make your hearts beat as one. You will begin to walk in the glory of the Lord, under His anointing power, with the authority He gives you. You will begin the transformation from the foot soldier of God, to the warrior He wants you to be. In doing so, you will be empowered to walk out the destiny to which He has called you.

Praying for yourself, crying out to God for this transformation is not selfish. It is one of the most beneficial and beautiful things you can do for God, for your family, and for all the hurting people around you. So dear Reader, come, break forth into an incredible journey to take new land. Pray with me the cry of my heart, taken from the first month of my journal, as I started on my true journey of faith with God. Then start giving Him the beatings of your own heart every day. I pray that by crying out to Him, He will take you to new spiritual levels beyond your imaginings!

Break Forth

Dear Heavenly Father,

Keep me focused on You, Lord. I am Yours. I long for intimacy with You. Help me give You the time! Let Your favor shine on Me, O Lord! Hide me in the shelter of Your presence. Help my heart and mind be open, and plant Your desires within me. Thank You for developing in me a deep reliance on You. Show me, O Lord, what You are doing in my life. Help me expect great things, but let my expectations be in line with Your will. Let me know Your heart, so I know Your will. Help me trust You in the dark, and not be discouraged. I want to see Your power and glory at work in all the negative situations in my life. I don't know what to ask or think ... show me ...

Help me trust You fully so You can fill me with Your peace and joy. Please give me a vision and a direction for my life. Show me my path. Lead me in the direction of life You would have me go. Restore my brokenness and my broken relationships in a way that is pleasing to You, without unhealthy compromise. Help me trust You with all my relationships. Help me see the situations from Your perspective. I will stop trying to figure it all out. Guide me in what I need to do to keep healing. Help me to stay in Your peace by trusting You. Help my desires be in line with Your will for my life. Help my desires come from knowing Your heart, and help me walk in Your presence. Help me to be the best "me" I can be.

Break Forth

Help me to recognize and to realize my inadequacies. Fill them in with Your grace, might and power. Help me lean on You in all areas. Fill my heart with Your love for me and for others.

Help me stop trying to think my way through trials ahead of time. I only want to go through them once, with You. Help me trust that You will give me the words to say, when I need to say them, and leave things I should not say, in all the situations I face. Help me relax in Your peace. Strengthen and prepare me for the day. Transform any fear, doubt and worry into Your confident hope and confident trust. Lord, help me not to be discouraged.

Father God, help me through all the scary circumstances I am facing. Help me understand what You want me to understand, and let go of what I will not. Help me reprogram the trauma patterns in my brain, and make them healthy. Show me what to pray. Help me live above my circumstances. Help me trust in You absolutely in all areas. Help me to pray the will of the Father, by knowing You. Help me pray with authority. Heal me, Lord, from any unmet needs of love and affection. Thank You for my chains, Lord, because my fight against them has made me strong in You, and has made me rely on You.

Help me keep every thought captive. Help me keep my eyes on You. I will follow You, one step at a time! Help me not be anxious about things that may or may not happen. I know You will be with me and that will make all the difference.

Break Forth

Let me be open to Your leading! Your ways are not my own. You will push me gently; in ways I would not think to go on my own. Your timing is amazing, and Your challenges guide me to fully trust You. I trust You to equip me for any mountains I must scale. Help me see each opportunity You put in my path, each word You guide me to say. Help my attitudes stay joyful, even when trials are at hand. I know You want to impact Your people daily. Let me be Your vessel to reach lives and touch hearts; those close to me, and those I do not know. I know I can't do this when my attitude is grumpy, sullen or depressed. Help me walk in joy, love and peace. Thank You for being my shelter. Your wings cover me. Thank You for Your promises which are my armor and protection. You are my shield. Help me to make You and You alone my shelter.

Renew my mind, O Lord. Help me to focus on You, rather than on my problems and circumstances. Keep my focus positive. Help me, Father, not to waste my time. Every moment of life is so precious. Attitude is everything. Overwhelm me with Your presence. I want to feel You in everything. You will give us all we need.

Transform my mind, O Lord, so my mind and my will become Your own. Please, Lord, change the way I think. Show me my gifts and help me use them to bring You glory.

Break Forth

Help me pray for and bless those who persecute me. Help me see all people as You see them.

O Father, give me eyes to see Your people. Show me ways to bless them and help them. Change my attitudes. Help me grow and change to become more like You; more pleasing and honoring to You. I repent where I have failed You in this area. I am humbled and honored that You have chosen me for Your servant, and for the many blessings You have given me. You are my lover and my husband, O Lord. I give You my heart, my loneliness, my finances, my hope, my restoration. Oh dance with me, Oh Lord, lover of my soul. Let my life unfold according to Your will, Your plan. I release my own will to Yours. I am surrendered to You and Your will for my life. Guide me, use me, show me, love me. My hope belongs to You. Show me and help me walk with You in all I do. Help me put my hopes and dreams in You. You are truly the author of the world and the author of hearts. Hear my pleas, O Lord. In Jesus' name!

Break Forth

Don't worry about anything; instead, pray about everything. Tell God what you need, and thank him for all he has done. Then you will experience God's peace, which exceeds anything we can understand. His peace will guard your hearts and minds as you live in Christ Jesus.
Philippians 4:6-7

Rejoice in our confident hope.
Be patient in trouble, and keep on praying.
Romans 12:12

And when he took the scroll, the four living beings and the twenty-four elders fell down before the Lamb. Each one had a harp, and they held gold bowls filled with incense, which are the prayers of God's people.
Revelations 5:8

Break Forth

Dear Child,

    Trust without borders. That is what I am leading you to. Trust with all your heart. Trust … dependence … hope—all born out of time with Me, learning about My heart for people, for you. Trust in My will for your life. You have authority in your prayers because it comes from being in My will. You are praying the heart of God, My heart, and that gives you power and authority. I will still guide you. Step by step, walk out in My power, with My grace, O warrior princess, and take others with you. Hold their hands as I have held yours.

♥ Jesus

Chapter Eleven

Life Changing Words

I LOVE JOURNALS … THE MANY DIFFERENT LOOKS, THE SMELL OF A new one, the feel of the page against my hand. I had purchased many of them over the years. But when reality speaks, I would enthusiastically write for a few days, and then quit. Every time something new and exciting introduced itself into my life, I'd buy a new journal to record the momentous occasion. Birthdays and New Years were no exceptions. Periodically I'd get more faithful, but I had yet to actually fill a whole journal until my life became nasty. At that point, I had to record things to keep myself out of denial and to provide a private sounding board to keep me sane. But even that was sporadic at best, usually surfacing when I was at one of my many breaking points.

I'm thankful that I did write. It provided the silent scream I needed. And later, as I wrote *Walking Tall*, my journals served as a template to the little broken girl I once was; the one who could reach right into the hearts of the other broken ones and say, "Yes, I understand what you are going through. I have been there too." When I wrote all those explicit words and

Break Forth

thoughts in my journals, I never, ever would have imagined they would become public. Nor would I have fathomed I would ever tell my story to the world in such graphic detail. But that was exactly what God asked me to do, and I am trusting people will be healed because of it.

When I look back over my old journals, filled with horrible things, I still get emotional, thinking of all she (me, when I was her) went through; how hollow and hopeless she felt. But isn't it just like our amazing God to be so detailed in His redemption of our lives? He can and will redeem everything. On January 1, 2015, He began a new work of transformation in me through the use of a journal. (I would have definitely picked a nicer one had I known how profound that first journal would become in my life!) Now, as I look at the new stack of journals (I'm on my twelfth in sixteen months)—each page a precious treasure that stirs awe and excitement in my heart—I cannot help but grin, shake my head and marvel at how the Lord truly does strategically redeem everything in our lives.

In previous years, I had been using my journal to record any prophetic words given to me and to write out the scriptures I felt particularly spoke to my heart. But generally, my communication with God had been an unscripted monologue. So, when my friend revealed that she had a dialogue with God during her times with Him, I was fascinated. Could I too, hear directly from the Almighty on a consistent basis?

I had been reading the devotional *Jesus Calling*[4] I had received mid-year from a friend for my birthday. However, as the calendar flipped over with the new year, I had the traditional desire to be more consistent and intentional in spending time with God. As I am a cover-to-cover type of learner, I opened my devotional to the introduction section, and finally, after many months of having it, I read of how it came to be. The author, inspired by the "listeners" in the devotional *God Calling*[5], decided she too, would write down

Break Forth

what she felt God was saying to her personally, as she communed with Him. After I read that, I just knew this was the awaited answer to my dialogue dilemma. I understood deep in my heart that I too, was to wait before the Lord, pen in hand, and begin to not only really listen, but to capture my journey of faith with Him on paper.

I started by reading the devotional and writing a prayerful response. Then I read the whole chapter for each of the included scriptures, and recorded any of them that strongly resonated within me. And then I was quiet, and listened, unsure of what to expect. At first, I didn't hear words exactly, but more felt them, as if they were impressed upon me, phrased in a way that was different than when I speak to myself. Words would then come to my mind, and I would just write them down, sometimes not even sure of where a sentence was going. There were only a few words or sentences at first, or nothing at all ... then a paragraph. But after I was "released," (see "Released to Write," in *Walking Tall*) a flood would come, sometimes filling pages that I would have to go back and read to see what was there.

I questioned God as to whether I was just writing my own heart, but He would faithfully bring people to me with words from the Lord, or scriptures that would replicate the words in my journal. Time and time again my words from the Lord would be confirmed, and I began to believe them. As the months passed, the words became more revelatory and the instructions more specific. It was as if He was giving me an instruction manual on how to walk with Him. He started giving me words and scriptures for others, and He taught me how to pray for them. Essentially, He taught me how we were to do life together as a unified community of believers.

It was through His words to me in my journal that I discovered fear was holding me back from releasing His very plan and destiny for my life. Fear was keeping me from writing what I knew by then I was called to write

Break Forth

—my story. It was through this communication from Him that He taught me many of the things I am now called to share with you. I began to realize why He had asked me to faithfully record my journey of healing and faith. At the time, although I saw myself as just a trauma survivor, still weak and needy, He saw me differently. "A warrior in the making" was what He called me, and I was to write it all, so I could share it all; in effect, linking arms with all of you, taking you with me into the ranks of His Heavenly Army.

As I sat down to write in that first journal just seventeen short months ago, I had no idea such a simple act would so radically change my life. It seems so much longer than that as I reflect back on all that has happened. That time in His presence each day became my lifeline—it still is. I now truly understand what it means to abide in the Lord. As my hunger grew during those early months, I had to keep setting my alarm clock for an earlier and earlier time, so I could linger in His presence a little longer. Even then it was hard to drag myself away without my spirit crying out that it was not enough time! Now God has even redeemed time for me, but that will be in another book!

The words God gave me in those times were truly life changing, and that still continues on an almost daily basis. I share this with you not so you'll try to replicate my journey. Everyone hears from the Lord so differently. I am a scribe; this is how I hear. But I do share this journey with you to encourage you to take the time—really take the time—to explore and understand how you hear from God, and to give Him the time He needs and wants so He can bring you closer to His heart. When you hear the Father's heart, it changes everything. Amazing things happen.

For years I had justified myself, truly believing I did not have any length of time available to spend with the Lord one on one. "I'm a busy university student ... a tired young mom ... I have two jobs ... I'm a single par-

Break Forth

ent …" Every stage of life seemed to bring with it a lack of time, impeding any worthwhile investment in the Lord. On good days I'd spend a few minutes at night in my devotional or my Bible and say some prayers, but for much of the time I was only multi-tasking throughout the day, sending brief prayers out as situations arose, along with participating in corporate services, prayer times, events and the like.

I still do those things, but now that I can somewhat conceive the depth of relationship we can share with the Lord, and the breadth of knowledge, revelation and gifts He wants to pour out on us as we push closer to Him, I will never again exchange this time in His presence for anything. Once we understand what the Lord God Almighty actually has for us in this lifetime, as opposed to what so many of us may have settled for, for what I had settled for during all those years … it changes everything.

At the time of this writing, I single-parent two active children, I teach full time, I am on several ministry teams, and I will have written two books within a one year period. And recently, God has opened the door to another opportunity—I am now helping others write their stories of God and life and love. And my house still gets cleaned, though not perfectly, my dishes get done most days, and we all have clean clothes to wear. Admittedly, some things slip through the cracks, but it all eventually gets taken care of. I take time to paint, exercise, coffee with my friends, attend workshops and plant all my flowers in spring. All of these things come after spending my precious time with Him bright and early in the morning. He is my priority, ahead of everything else in my day. He then orders my day. And then I am able to do more than what seems humanly possible. And it is not humanly possible, yet I do, because with God, all things are possible (Matthew 19:26).

There are no reasons or excuses big enough to justify us short-circuiting the promises He has for us, if we only draw near. There will be seasons in

Break Forth

your life where you spend more time with Him, and others, less. But I encourage you, implore you, urge you … seek the Lord with *all* your heart. Truly seek Him. You will not regret it. The adventure He takes you on will be beyond your wildest dreams. It will be His dreams. I do encourage you to record the things God speaks to you. It is beyond-words-amazing to see your journey progress, and to go back and drink in over and over, all the things He is feeding your soul. Some of the things He speaks are for now, and some for later, in preparation for things to come. A record of those things can help guide you through the unknown paths before you. Words for others around you too, may appear, and as these ones start seeking answers, you may already be holding those words in your hand that will ease their hearts. It will change their lives. And yours. You will see His glory manifest, and it will change everything. Come now, I would like the honor of praying with you, just Holy Spirit and me. It will change everything.

Dear Holy Father,

    My heart can barely contain my joy as I have come to understand all You have for each one of us. I know in whom I trust, and I ask You, Lord, to show my friends how to know You more. It is in truly knowing You and loving You that we can be changed. So now I ask You, Father, to break off any lies of the enemy that are telling my friends that there is no more time to spend in Your presence, or that the investment of time will not be worth it or change anything. Let them know deep in their hearts, Lord, that learning to hear more of Your voice and taking the time that is truly needed to develop the relationship with You to the depth You desire, is priceless. It is the trea-

Break Forth

sure they seek and the only thing that will bring life changing words into their hearts and minds. Help them to understand that it is more important than any other thing You have called us to do. Help them understand that it will not only change them, but it will also have incredible impact on everyone's lives around them, as it will spill God's glory over onto everyone they encounter. Lord God, as they seek You, please give them the life changing words they desire. Multiply their time in unimaginable ways, showering them with Your blessings, as they are faithful in pursuing You. In Jesus' name, I pray this. Now it is your turn.

Dear Lord,

Thank You for wanting to know me, and desiring that I know You more. Help me develop such an intimate relationship with You that I can hear Your very heartbeat. Forgive me for all the times in my past that I chose to do other things rather than to spend time with You. Show me how to order my day so You will be my first love and my first priority. Teach me to hear Your voice ever more clearly. Show me what my journey of faith looks like. Reveal to me all the ways You operate in my life. Open the eyes of my understanding so I may know You more. Bring about the changes in my life so it is pleasing to You, and so I am open

Break Forth

and available to You to do all You ask of me, and to become all You desire me to become. Teach me to be obedient in spending time with You. Teach me how to be in Your presence, and to daily seek You. Impress it on my heart, so I understand how precious my relationship with You truly is. I ask for a heart of revelation of the treasure I have available through You if only I honestly seek You to the depth of my being. Show me what that actually means, and how it can come to be in my life. Help me with this, God. Lord, I offer my life and my time as a living sacrifice unto You. Thank You that this is the way You desire it to be. I bless Your holy name. I pray this in the power of Jesus' name. Amen.

> Jesus replied, " 'You must love the LORD your God with all your heart, all your soul, and all your mind.' This is the first and greatest commandment.
> *Matthew 22:37-38*

Break Forth

> I pray that from his glorious, unlimited resources, he will empower you with inner strength through his Spirit. Then Christ will make his home in your hearts as you trust in him. Your roots will grow down into God's love and keep you strong. And may you have the power to understand, as all God's people should, how wide, how long, how high, and how deep his love is.
> *Ephesians 3:16-18*

> Don't you realize that in a race everyone runs, but only one person gets the prize? So run to win! All athletes are disciplined in their training. They do it to win a prize that will fade away, but we do it for an eternal prize. So I run with purpose in every step. I am not just shadowboxing. I discipline my body like an athlete, training it to do what it should. Otherwise, I fear that after preaching to others I myself might be disqualified.
> *1 Corinthians 9:24-27*

Break Forth

Oh My Child,

    Life is found in My presence. There is no other life that can compare. There is no exchange for time in My presence; no short-cut, no unpaid withdrawl. Time with Me is life giving. As you come to understand this principle, your life will change, your attitude will change, your priorities will change. There is no other source of such pure power, than time spent with Me. I will open the world to your understanding, as you sit at My feet like a child at the feet of a wise one. I will pour out My love on you, as you pour out your love to Me. I will exchange every place of tears of sorrow, for tears of joy and gratefulness, as you humble yourself before Me, and put up your hands. As you learn to walk with Me daily, I will unveil the earth so you walk among the stars in the light of day. My light shines ever before you, beckoning you to come. Let My light fill every place of you, fill you with My presence. There is no other way. Let My Holy Spirit surround you as you sit quietly before Me, waiting, listening, learning, drinking Me in. It is then that your heart will be able to pour out to all the thirsty people who so need to find Me, find My love. Come, be with Me, and I will give you the world.

                                               ♥ God the Father

Chapter Twelve

Praying for Your Enemies

I WROTE THE FOLLOWING SECTION AS A PART OF A TEACHING I GAVE at a retreat this year. God always manages to arrange things so perfectly ... placing the right topic into the hands of His people ...

Planting the Seeds of Fear

As the sounds of erupting anger and the ensuing screams and crashes come rushing down the hallway from the other room, I can only imagine how the little boy responds ... maybe his tiny hands cover his ears, or maybe they are clutching the covers and pulling them up over his head to dull the sound of flesh on flesh coming from the other room. Or maybe he is hiding under his bed or in the closet, trying to find some semblance of safety and to keep the horror from imprinting on his mind as the sounds of anger filter in and fill his room.

I can only imagine his response, but I have no doubt of the result. A deep fear has wrapped itself around his little heart and a sense of all control is lost. Maybe hard walls soon rise up around him, so the dents in the walls and the broken things and the broken hearts of daily life no longer send him crumbling in on himself. The pain was too hard to bear for his little body, so he was grateful for the ability to turn cold and hard when he felt he had to. Having been left on his own to deal with the pain and suffering, he did the best he could. But the only tool he had was a shovel, as he tried to bury it all as deeply as he could, never, he vowed, to surface. But deep down within the heart of stone, his heart of flesh still beat … full of fear and full of wounds … it still beat.

Flash forward many years. The heart of stone and wounded flesh have constructed a lifestyle of such contradiction that it is impossible for him to attain any peace. The gaping holes in his heart, without healing, could never be filled. Nothing was ever enough. Never enough love, respect, money, hope, gratitude, perfection, peace … Nothing seemed to fill the insatiable needs in his heart. So he set out to control the environment, circumstances and people around him, trying to jam them into his heart in the right way to plug the needs and stop it from perpetually leaking, and to stop the pain which still numbed his whole being, and to stifle the fear which constantly threatened to overtake him still.

But as he met resistance from the environment, the circumstances, and especially the people who refused him, anger arose. And more anger. And

Break Forth

more anger ... always escalating, always more anger needed as those around him—his brother, his sister, his wife, and then his kids—no longer responded with a jump to attention as they once did with only a few angry words, a harsh tone, and maybe a fist raised for effect. So the anger kept rising and rising ... and then finally began to explode. The destruction began, sending the shrapnel of fear into the souls of those little bodies as they ran away from him, and as the tears ran down their cheeks and into their hearts and once again planted and watered the seeds of fear ... and so the cycle goes. ☹

This is not a fictitious story. I am part of it. I know these people—they are so dear to my heart. You know these people too. They are dear to your heart ... and maybe it is your own heart too. But it doesn't have to be this way. Today we want to give you more tools than just a shovel to bury your pain. We want to give you the tools to break the chains of fear, anger and control. We want to give you Jesus to heal your heart to the depths of your being so the fear and its ugly cohorts will be banished and you will be free from all their grave effects.

The story is based on abuse planting the seeds of fear, but it is not only living in abuse that plants seeds of fear. It can be so many things; any form of trauma that places unhealthy fear in your heart that torments, binds and inhibits.

In my own life, fear was planted so deep in my heart by the words spoken over me and the abuse perpetuated against me that I was ruled by it. I was very fear-based in many of my decisions. Fear was blocking me from stepping out in some of the things God had called me to do ... trying to thwart my destiny. My body became hyper-vigilant down to the cellular level, and caused a lot of pain and sickness. But God says, "Perfect love casts out fear." God loves you and it is His will for you to be free from tormenting fear.

Break Forth

Fear, anger and control ... they were so well known to me. I was easily able to speak from my heart on this topic, and then lead the participants through the specific information and cleansing prayers, giving them the tools to heal and break the chains. But for where I was in my journey, it provided a totally different and completely unexpected tool.

As I wrote about this little boy with the breaking and wounded heart, I wept continually. In preparation for my teaching, I could not read it through without compassion rising up in me. The tears continued to flow freely. I honestly wept in heartbreak for that little boy ... the same little boy who grew up to be the man with the hard heart who attempted to destroy me; that same man for whom I had little compassion. No, I could not pray for that man in spirit and in truth. But for that little boy ... I wept. He touched my heart to the very core. For him, I could cry. For him, I could pray, to the depths of my soul.

Praying for the man he is now did not come instantly. It was a process, and at first I still needed the support of my prayer warrior friends. Some days, I still do. But something inside of me broke that day, and I realized that God had handed me the key to praying for my enemies. I began to see the man that he was in his woundedness, covered up with layer upon layer of protective personalities in attempts to keep himself from breaking. I began to see him as God sees him ... and I was finally able to pray for him in spirit and in truth.

I still have to continually ask God to help me see Rob as He sees him. As incident piles upon incident, I need to remind myself of where he came from and why he is the way he is. I do have to fight through exasperation and anger as to why, now an adult, he could not/would not face the truth and pain of his life, which would bring about his own healing. But I have no control over that, and can only offer it up to God as well, and pray for a breakthrough in his healing.

But, in being able to pray for Rob, I have become more true to who I am. I have become closer to being like Christ, and am able to walk the way God wants me to walk, without the roots of vengeance, bitterness and hatred growing in my heart. As hard as it is, praying for the one who hurts me uproots many of the unhealthy things that could grow in my heart, and it prevents new roots from taking hold. It also helps me to again realize that Rob is not the real enemy, but only a pawn in the scheme of the true enemy of my soul.

So now, dear Reader, I hand you the key to praying for your enemies. It is a heavy thing to ask of one so wounded and broken, I know. But forgiving and praying for your enemies releases an incredible freedom in your heart that otherwise would be left heavy and burdened. So just ask God to help you see them as He sees them. Ask God to give you the compassion for them you do not have—you cannot manufacture on your own, without the power of Holy Spirit. It may take time and persistence for this breakthrough, and you have to be ready. But God will give it to you if you want it, or even want to want it. And it may come in an amazing and surprising way. By learning to pray for your enemies, you are setting yourself free from captivity—free to walk as the child of God He has intended you to be. Come kneel with us. Come before the Lord of Hosts and ask Him to help you with this monumental step in your healing.

Break Forth

Lord God,

Sometimes I feel like everything I have been through has taken so much away from me. The wounding goes deep. It even changed who I was, and who I am. But Lord, thank You for wanting such a deep healing for my heart that You are not satisfied until every part of it is free. I know that as painful as it is, I need to forgive those who hurt me, in order for complete freedom to come into my own life. I do not want to carry any of it any more. I know that what happened to me was not right. It was not just. It was not fair. But Lord, You know this too. My forgiveness of them does not say what they did was okay. It does condone what they did, but just leaves them in Your hands instead of mine, and Yours are much more capable of dealing with all of it than mine. And thank You, Lord, that it then releases me to heal.

So Lord, I repent of all unforgiveness, and I ask that by the power of Holy Spirit, I can truly forgive. I know if I first confess it with my mouth, with Your help, my heart will then follow, and I will truly forgive. I know this will then leave more room in my heart for peace.

Break Forth

So Lord, right now I forgive _____ for _____. I pray for Your grace, Your mercy, Your support, and Your justice to flow.

Now Lord, with Your help, I want to take it a step further. I want to truly be the warrior You are calling me to be. Your word says to pray for those who hurt you; pray for those who persecute you, and I want to be obedient.

You, Lord Jesus, were hurt and persecuted beyond measure, but You prayed for the ones who claimed to be Your enemy. Help me be more like You. Help me pray for mine.

(Adapt the following prayer as needed.) So Lord, I bring _____ before you. Please change my attitude toward the one I call my enemy. Help me to see him not as the enemy, but see him as you do. Please give me a compassion for him beyond my capabilities. Help me see him as the child he once was—broken and hurting. Please release Your power upon him so that he may be healed from all his affliction. Please help him let go of the anger, hurt, control, confusion, abuse and trauma that has ruled him for so long.

Change the ingrained patterns, reactions and habits that have formed in his thought process. Lord God, in Jesus' name, I ask You to wash away the pain that causes him to lash out at the world around him, and at all those in his life.

Break Forth

Please put gentleness where there has been anger. Put understanding where there has been challenge. Bring comfort to his heart where there has been pain. In Jesus' name, replace all the evil things that have taken root and grown in the heart of this man, with the love and humility You desire. Bind up any pride, and replace his heart of stone with one of flesh. Bring a deep healing into his life so he can go forth and see You, put his faith in You, and be the man of God You desire him to be. Bless him, Lord. Touch him. Help him to receive Your love.

Thank You, Lord, for giving me the strength to pray for those that hurt me. In doing so, You are healing my heart, making it new, and raising me up to be the one You are calling me to be. Thank You for caring so much about me that You would lead me so gently and carefully through something as painful as this. I give all the glory to Your name, Lord Jesus. Amen.

Break Forth

> He did not retaliate when he was insulted,
> nor threaten revenge when he suffered. He
> left his case in the hands of God, who
> always judges fairly.
> *1 Peter 2:23*

> "You have heard the law that says, 'Love your
> neighbor' and hate your enemy. But I say,
> love your enemies! Pray for those who perse-
> cute you! In that way, you will be acting as
> true children of your Father in heaven. For he
> gives his sunlight to both the evil and the
> good, and he sends rain on the just and the
> unjust alike.
> Matthew 5:43-45

> But to you who are willing to listen, I say,
> love your enemies! Do good to those who
> hate you. Bless those who curse you. Pray
> for those who hurt you.
> *Luke 6:27-28*

Break Forth

> Bless those who persecute you. Don't curse them; pray that God will bless them.
> *Romans 12:14*

Oh My Child,

    Let the sorrow go; that sorrow that binds you. Be still in My presence and let it wash over you. I will heal those deep places of your heart that harbor all those things keeping you from Me, keeping you from the joy I want released in your life—need released in your life. I did not intend for you to walk through all the pain of the past and bring it into the future. That is not My walk for you. Let go, My Child. The lies that grip your heart in ice can be released as you hear My voice and allow Me in to calm that storm. It is real, Child. I know you feel your fear is real, but make Me more real. Allow My love to be more real than the fear that enslaves you. Believe on Me, My Child … this is what I ask of you. I know it takes strength, but I will give you the strength you need. Trust Me, Child, trust Me … and let go.

♥ Jesus

Chapter Thirteen

The Most Amazing Horrible Day

I WANT TO GO HOME! MY MIND CRIED, AS AN OVERWHELMING DREAD crept over me. Minutes from now I would be called up to minister on the prayer line at the Cleansing Stream[6] retreat. Bone tired and feeling in over my head, I knew, however, going home was not an option. As the tremendous breakthrough came to the ones I prayed with that session, it was then I realized those feelings were, in fact, a devious spiritual attack.

The night before, when the random, outrageous thought, *I should just kill myself,* popped into my brain in the middle of the grocery store, I pretty much scoffed at the enemy. Being nowhere near that frame of mind, I knew it was an attack because of the retreat in which I would be ministering. But this "I want to go home" attack was much more subtle ... believable. I was being deceived by this one. Only later would God reveal that the enemy had already used this approach several times with me, and even tried to avert a huge breakthrough in my healing with it. But as always, my faithful God turned it on its head. The following account describes how He used this very attack to put another precious weapon against the enemy in my arsenal.

Most of my adult life I had been nervous about traveling anywhere more than a few hours away by myself. I have inherited my dad's complete lack of directional sense rather than my mom's built-in GPS. Wrong turns, driving in circles, mounting anxiety, fear of never finding the right place, and tears of frustration were a regular part of my road trip routine. But God wanted to break that fear off of me by having me finally face it. However, a seemingly God-ordained trip to Calgary fell through, after I already had promised a friend who lived there I'd be seeing her soon. Then, in its stead, the opportunity to go to a women's retreat hosted by Kimberly McEwen of Hearts on Fire Ministries[7] presented itself. Overcoming my fear, a Spirit-filled, fun-filled event, and seeing a great friend after a lot of years were all bundled together. I anticipated an amazing weekend!

And an amazing weekend it was ... incredible worship and speakers, prophetic words, a free candy bar, spa treatments. But in the midst of it, I had a breakdown and wanted desperately to go home. This was so unlike me, as normally I thrive on these sorts of events. But as I stood off to the side watching others receive their prophetic foot massages, I had angry black walls surrounding me, covering me, pulsing through me, making me feel like I would lash out at anyone who dared come near me, or, God forbid, touched me.

A prophetic word given the night before spoke of someone who desperately wanted to look up and see Jesus, but was being blocked. This was supposed to be her weekend of freedom. I had cried when I heard it. I thought that meant that word was for me. But here I was, at the most amazing retreat, with the most amazing people ... and having the most awful time. The only thing I wanted was to go home. It should have been the perfect weekend, but my response was not what I had anticipated nor expected. And the strange part was that I did not even remotely understand what on earth was going on with me, nor why I was feeling this way. I even had reverted to old behaviors of distancing myself from others and having to keep my back to the wall, not allowing anyone to be behind me, in order to feel safe.

Mid afternoon and a mess, I counted the hours left in the day to see if the long drive home was still feasible. Becoming aware of my increasing distress, my friend ran interference for me, and after talking to Kimberley, arranged a divine appointment with the speaker, Brenda Peters. Her first prophetic word of my overtaxed immune system would eventually be more than confirmed. (Five months later, doctors, neurology and a CT scan would enter the scene as I tried to discover why my head was in constant pain and why my body was shutting down.) Next, a brief history of my past was recounted. Then prayers and her spiritual discernment determined that I had an assignment against me from the enemy. Ensuring me I had to take the reins in this, she taught me how to break off this assignment and future assignments against me as quickly as I recognized them. This became an immensely valuable tool as I continue to face the giants that rise up against me.

As I rejoined the women at the retreat after the prayer session with Brenda, I was unrecognizable. They had only met me with that shroud of ugliness over me, and were amazed to see "a whole new countenance." This was actually the real me, but only my friend knew that. With the assignment and its hold over me broken, I was able to "look up and see Jesus," and receive for the remainder of the weekend. I no longer wanted to go home. Finally feeling safe, I had the opportunity to share my testimony, and for the first time publicly talk about the abuse that had ruled my life for so long.

Break Forth

Since only two people in the room even knew my last name, I did not feel the deep need for secrecy to hide my past. I had a feeling, even then, that one day I would again be bringing my story into the light for the purposes of God.

Since then, I have learned that assignments put on you by the enemy can be aggressive, such as suicidal or murderous thoughts, or more subtle, discouraging ones that make you want to leave or run. There can be emotional assignments such as anger, mistrust, resentment, depression, despair and hate. There can also be physical attacks such as dizziness, distraction, confusion, and infirmity. Gag orders can be put on you to steal your voice, and walls of silence can be built around you. Perverse thoughts, images and dreams can be sent to invade your mind and produce guilt and condemnation if you begin to believe they are a part of you. A bully spirit can be set against you to intimidate and instill fear. Deception can try to thwart your destiny.

The attacks can come tangled in with nasty circumstances, hiding their existence, or on their own, seemingly out of context and making no sense. Sometimes it takes me days to recognize what I think are my emotions or a physical ailment, as an attack. Other times I see them in an instant, like the now familiar wave of sudden dizziness and blurred vision at the moment of trying to send a God-inspired text to a friend, before a designated prayer time, or during an intense conversation that threatens to reveal an enemy tactic. But because of this awareness of how the enemy operates, I can now break off these attacks before they have a chance to even settle over my body and enter my soul. Sometimes I can break these assignments off on my own, but other times it seems to require another to pray over me.

When I came back from the retreat that weekend, I was no longer frustrated by my lack of participation, for though I had missed out in some ways, what I had gained in spiritual warfare tools far outweighed anything else. The Lord, through His grace and goodness, gave me revelation of the

Break Forth

intense damage an enemy attack can inflict on a person. It can come on so strong and hard it literally stops our ability to function, let alone receive anything from God, or from anyone else. I was blessed to have had such wise and godly people around me that day, and most days since, to pull me out from under it, and to teach me how to counter attack and enlist God's protection over me. I am not being over-dramatic when I say I shudder to think of what would have happened to me over the course of my lifetime, had I not been freed from it that weekend, or from the many attacks since then that would have piled up over me, suffocating all that God was trying to birth in me.

The sad part is that I do not have to look very far to see the reality of what it looks like. I see so many of the walking wounded, the emotionally bleeding and dying all around me, even in the church. The years of attacks, without constant cleansing, weigh heavily on their souls and keep them from being the radiant bride of Christ that draws all men unto the Father. How can we shine with the glory of God when we are covered with layer upon layer of filth from the enemy?

My prayer team sees this prophetic picture over you: I can see God raising you up and calling you out. But the enemy wants to put all these blocks in front of you. I can see you walking through what is almost like an obstacle course. You'll be walking into a room and out of nowhere comes a wall or something else to trip you up. I want you to see that these are the assignments that the enemy puts against you. But you have the authority to remove them by the power of Jesus' name.

So let's put on the armor of God and break free from the assignments put on you by calling on the name of Jesus and the finished work of the cross. (Adapt the prayer as needed.)

Break Forth

Dear Heavenly Father,

Thank You for showing me that the enemy uses specific assignments against me to come between me and You, my Lord. I see how he loves to put another box over me, to add another ceiling or impose something, anything that will attempt to prevent me from stepping out, speaking out and walking into the will, the plans, and the purposes You have set for me. Please help me identify quickly and easily each trap, hindrance and assignment the enemy uses against me, whether it be an obstruction, trying to prevent me from getting where You want me to be, a physical or emotional attack straight from the deceiver himself, or an attack from another used as a pawn of the enemy.

Lord, I pray I can recognize it for what it is, and that You will help me to press through so I can receive all You have planned for me in that moment. It is in these times, I know, that there is something special You have for me. Perhaps it is a powerful breakthrough, a revelation, or a sweet time of intimacy with You as You speak deep into my heart and set me free in yet another area of my life. Lord, help me to understand that anger, strife, anxiety and fear are favorite tools of the enemy to try to stop me in my tracks; to prevent me from functioning in the peace and joy You have intended. I break those off in Jesus' name. Lord, thank You for exposing that internal struggles with depression and other mental illnesses may be attacks against me. I break those off in Jesus' name. Lord, if I am believing any lies, have made any vows, or have had any curses spoken over me that are enemy assignments against me, such as "I hate people," "I don't want to be here," "I will never/always…" or _____ (ask Holy Spirit to reveal any specific lies, vows or curses) I cancel that assignment right now by the power of the name of Jesus. Lord, I ask You right now to put a wall of protection around me and my family. Send your guardian angels to watch over us, and Your Holy Spirit to guide me.

Father God, there is power in speaking Your Word and Your truths out loud. The lies and deception lose their power as they are exposed and the truth is declared. So Lord, I break off any gag order put on me that tries to prevent me from speaking the truth, speaking out loud, and freely speaking my heart to You and others. I cancel this assignment by the power of the blood of Jesus.

Expose any lies I've believed in this area, such as, "I have nothing worthwhile to say," or "I have nothing to contribute."

Break Forth

Lord, I ask for all the tools and wisdom and revelation I will need to fight the good fight on the front lines of Your army. Help me be strong in You and in Your power. As I put on the armor You've assigned me in Ephesians 6, help me stand firm against all the strategies of the devil. Thank You for helping me understand that I am not fighting against flesh and blood enemies, but against evil rulers and authorities of the unseen world, against mighty powers in this dark world, and against evil spirits in heavenly places. Help me stand my ground as I put on the belt of truth and the body armor of God's righteousness. Lord, as I put on the peace that comes from the gospel, help me to be fully prepared.

I hold up the shield of faith to stop the fiery arrows of the enemy. I put on salvation as my helmet, protecting my mind. And I pick up my sword of the Spirit, which is the living, breathing Word of God. Help me to pray in the Spirit at all times and on every occasion. Oh Lord, keep me alert and persistent in my prayers.

In Your strength, Lord, I will be the radiant bride of Christ, walking in the joy, faith, freedom and peace You have ordained for my life before the ages. In Jesus' name, I humbly ask this of You. Amen.

Break Forth

Praise the LORD, who is my rock.
He trains my hands for war
and gives my fingers skill for battle.
He is my loving ally and my fortress,
my tower of safety, my rescuer.
He is my shield, and I take refuge in him.
He makes the nations submit to me.
O LORD, what are human beings that you should notice them,
mere mortals that you
should think about them?
For they are like a breath of air;
their days are like a passing shadow.
Open the heavens, LORD, and come down.
Touch the mountains so they billow smoke.
Hurl the lightning bolts and scatter your enemies!
Shoot your arrows and confuse them!
Reach down from heaven and rescue me;
rescue me from deep waters,
from the power of my enemies.

Psalm 144:1-7

Break Forth

My dear Child,

    Push back the lies that are invading your mind and taking over your soul. They threaten to drown out My voice and overtake you! Rest in Me. Focus on My presence. Focus on My breath blowing on your face. It is that still small voice whispering to your very soul that you need to tend to … not the blaring alarms that fight for your attention. Turn to Me in spirit and in truth. Ask Me. I long for My children to ask Me. I will be faithful in showing them the truth as they turn to Me in honesty and truth, with their hearts exposed, and ask. I will reveal all the secrets of the universe to you, Child, as you seek Me. Do not be deceived. I put the truth deep into your heart. It will not be moved. It will not be removed. It needs to be watered and nurtured and then it will grow, becoming louder and stronger as you walk faithfully with Me. Put it off no longer, Child. Stretch out your hand to Me and I will fill it with the truth. You will know, My Child, you will know.

Trust …

♥ Jesus

Chapter Fourteen

Just Another Chapter

I COLLAPSED TO THE FLOOR IN MY CLASSROOM, MY LEGS UNABLE TO hold me up any longer. In tears, I tried to wrap my mind around the reality that I may no longer be able to keep teaching, or do anything else, for that matter. I had taught for almost twenty years, and as a single parent, it was my family's sole means of support. My doctor told me to get my papers in order in the likely case I would have to go on disability. I recognized how close I had come to being mentally and emotionally broken almost beyond repair, but I had no idea the toll it had taken on my body. It was just now starting to show up ... now, after I finally had gotten back up on my feet mentally, emotionally and spiritually.

"Lord!" I cried. "My spring is supposed to be here! I have worked so hard and healed so much! Why is this happening now? I already have a story! I don't need another one!"

Break Forth

"Calli, My dear, it's not another story ... it is the same story ... just another chapter ..."

The strangest sensation came across my head while I was in my classroom that day in March. It was like something swept across my brain from the right side of my head to the middle, completely distorting my vision. It stalled my thoughts and functions and stole my bearings. I wasn't sure if I could keep standing. My vice-principal happened to be walking by as I struggled to figure out what to do. Glad to have someone pray for me and watch my class, I sat on the hard floor in the hallway, my mind racing as to what might be happening in my brain. Was this what a stroke felt like?

The sensation passed and my vision cleared, but I was left with a twenty-four-hour-a-day headache and a burning sensation in the back of my head. Frequent spikes of piercing pain would shoot through the left side of my head just above my temple. After many months of differing degrees of pain, doctor and neurologist appointments, a CT scan and pain medication that made my heart race (I quit taking it after the second dose), there was still no specific diagnosis. The neurologist suggested I suffered from a disease called "migraines" and recommended a more potent pain medication. After reading the side effects, I adamantly decided I would not risk blindness. Besides, something deep in my spirit knew there had to be a reason for my constant marathon headache of now five months. You do not just have pain without a source. Pain is a symptom, not a disease. If I masked only the symptom, the actual "thing" ravaging my body would continue to flourish.

Break Forth

I believe this was wisdom from the Lord, because a short time later I would visit a naturopathic doctor on the prairies that would finally be able to help. In the meantime, I would continue to deteriorate. The level of pain in my head continued to increase. It felt like a two-inch thick elastic band had wormed its way inside my skull and was squeezing my brain. I started getting strange dizzy spells which gave me the feeling I imagined people would experience as they time traveled or crossed into another dimension. I was experiencing a high level of constant nausea that made me want to crawl back into bed. The worst part came in the fall, when my body, completely overwhelmed, would impel my legs to give out and I would end up on my knees wherever I was. I was scared I could no longer function at work, in society, or in my own home. At this lowest point, only a few people knew how desperate I was becoming. I was scared for what the future could hold for me. If I did not have my children, I would have wished for the Lord to take me home.

The whole situation was humbling and very humiliating for me. I was always physically strong. I was proud of the toned muscles I had acquired from the years of being somewhat conscientious of keeping myself in shape. I had always been proficient in my job, keeping ahead of all my tasks, doing more than my fair share of extra curricular, and usually doing other department work or writing tasks on the side. Now here I was, having to take a sick day every week just to make it through, and unsure of how I would complete even the most basic tasks in my job, especially the ones involving the use of my computer. The pain level in my head would shoot through the roof when I tried. I did not seem to be able to even function around other people. I stayed away from church and most other public and private functions. If I really wanted to or had to attend, I would stand at the back of the room or off in a corner by myself. Taking care of my children took most of my limited energy. I literally could no longer even stand on my own two feet!

Break Forth

When I received prayer for this deterioration of my body and life, the disappointing word was that the Lord was not going to heal me immediately as I longed for, but I would have to walk through this one. *Oh great*, I had thought. The only reprieve was that by this time I had visited a naturopathic doctor who, with the help of a complex biofeedback analysis, told me what was going on in my body. Without the benefit of any of my medical records, he told me many things about my medical history I already knew, so when he told me about the things I did not know, I believed him. Summing it up, my body was so toxic it had begun to shut down. He deemed it wise to get disability papers in order. He didn't understand how I wasn't already in a wheelchair. I knew that if I didn't make some drastic changes, I soon would be.

This report made me so grateful to the Lord for my decision to skip the high-powered (highly toxic) pain medication and keep pursuing my healing in other avenues. Adding more toxic substances to filter through my overtaxed liver and store in my already over laden body would have been disastrous. This is exactly how life-ending diseases are created. How often we hear of someone fighting through and winning a stress-filled battle, only to be diagnosed with cancer or some other life-threatening disease.

Determined to turn things around, I embarked on the strict regimen the doctor gave me. I took Bio-Chelat to combat the high levels of metal that had somehow accumulated in my body. My unsolicited middle of the night and early morning waking routine, once a frustrating reality, became an asset. It provided me with the time periods I needed to take this detoxification product with the required two hours of fasting on both sides of the dosage, three times a day. (Though the inability to fall asleep until 6:00 a.m. at times, did take its toll in its own right.) The other supplements to fight the toxoplasmosis (dangerous to me because of my weakened immune system), yeast overgrowth in my digestive system, and depleted adrenal glands, became part

Break Forth

of my life several times a day. (I thank the Lord for my sister and brother-in-law who helped me pay for all the supplements.) My focus shifted from taking care of everyone else, to making my health a top priority.

My food intake became meat, vegetables, nuts, seeds and berries. I ate homemade and organic when possible. I learned to love making bone broth and jam; it reminded me of my grandma. I avoided restaurants and fast food. I did not eat wheat. I had known for years that my faulty thyroid was linked to an autoimmune disease, but I did not know this made me intolerant to gluten. I had to avoid grains, dairy, caffeine, sugar and most other natural sweeteners and high sugar fruit. I was to avoid anything processed or that contained additives or chemicals. Even tap water was crossed off my allowable list. A Berkey water filter, which claims to make even ditch water safe, was soon assembled, with only a minimal amount of frustration. The intent was to not consume any more things my body would consider toxic. This would give my overworked liver a chance to clear, and then it would allow the toxins being stored deep in my body—in the fat tissues, the connective tissues (ligaments, bones, blood, muscle, nerves), and right down to the cells and organs, to be cleansed. It was partly these toxins that were forcing my body to shut down. If I could just give it a chance, my body could heal itself. God designed our bodies to regenerate this way, when we stop abusing them.

Putting all these things into practice basically took over every aspect of my existence for a time. I felt like I was fighting for my life. I was—at least life as I knew it. Yet that was to be the easier part of my healing. The other part, according to the doctor, was more difficult to heal. The excessive adrenaline and cortisol spilling through me during all those years of trauma had been wreaking havoc not only on my soul, but on my body. Adrenaline prepares you for flight or to fight in a life-threatening situation by providing you with the necessary energy. When you neither fight nor flee to expend that energy, but instead you freeze (like I did), that mini tornado of energy gets trapped in your body and stored. Our bodies are not meant to be under the constant siege of trauma from abuse. Barring a complete description of the physiological responses in our bodies, the end result is far from healthy. What ends up happening, to the best of my knowledge and experience, is that your nervous system becomes hyper-vigilant, right down to the cellular level. Your body becomes on high alert to detect anything that may possibly be trying to harm it. That was part of the constant feeling I described in *Walking Tall*; the constant fear that something was "going to get me."

My somatic counselor explained it in this way: if you get hit by a baseball on the right side of your face, your body may become hyper-vigilant in one of two ways. You will either be hyper-vigilant to the right side, watching, waiting and expecting something else to come at you from that side again. Or, you will be hyper-vigilant to the left side, presumably seeking the safety of the absence of a traumatic experience. (Somatic experience counseling involves understanding how the body physiologically responds to trauma, and learning how to retrain it. Read Levine's book *Waking the Tiger*[8] for a detailed account.) It is as if your body becomes attuned to any potential danger. As this constant alertness detects potential danger, it sets off physiological responses—one of them being pain. The problem lies in that this hyper-vigilance is taken to extremes. It detects things that, under normal circumstances and with a healthy immune system, would not necessarily harm you.

My body had become hyper-vigilant to the cellular level, and what it was picking up as potential danger, was electro-magnetic radiation: the unseen waves in the air given off by high-voltage power lines, electrical panels, cell phone towers, cell phones, cordless phones, smart meters, Wi-Fi ... which would explain the constant headache. It is nearly impossible to be away from these things in today's society. For me, though I feel it was a form

Break Forth

of hypersensitivity, my body was protecting me, because radiation from those sources is filtered through your liver, and my body, in its weakened state, was just not able to filter the same amount as most people. (Though time will tell if this constant radiation is as safe as society believes it is.)

Either way, the doctor's confirmation that I was sensitive to electromagnetic radiation confirmed what I had already discovered through my own experiences and research. He gave me three directives to combat this condition. First, I had to avoid the sources of radiation as much as possible. I had to keep my cell phone on airplane mode to cut the signal. I would periodically turn airplane mode off so I could receive any texts or messages that had been sent, or to send a message of my own. I still do this. Though it is not overly convenient, it is much more so than not being able to function. Gone were Facebook and cell phone conversations. I disconnected my Wi-Fi and went back to wired Internet and a wired landline.

I kept avoiding public events and even people as much as possible, as the majority of them carried cell phones. My house church leader always asked people to turn off their phones so I could attend house church. I was so thankful for that. Teachers were also asked to do the same for staff meetings, as much as possible. I spent most of my lunch hours alone in my room, but when I did join the teachers in the staff room, they would switch to airplane mode when they saw me coming. I felt grateful they were accommodating me, but I also felt humiliated at the weakness of my body that required them to do this for me. I asked the teacher in the classroom next to me to keep her phone at the far end of her room. I could always tell when she forgot, as within half an hour I would be dropping to my knees in my room, and my head would be entering that other dimension.

I moved my bedroom down into the basement, farther away from my neighbor's Wi-Fi. As well, I installed Greenwave filters for the electrical out-

Break Forth

lets in my house and in my classroom, and I slept on grounding sheets to combat the radiation I had already accumulated in my body.[9] I purchased a meter that reads the electro-magnetic frequency (EMF), so I could find the best places in each building to spend my time. I was soon able to predict the reading it would give, just by the feeling in my head. My friends thought it was strange that I could feel the electricity and radiation around me, but their skepticism was proven wrong, as time and time again I could tell without even turning around, when the person behind me began to use their phone. I often felt like I was living in a science fiction movie. Sometimes I still do, only now it is more like *Star Trek* meets *The Chronicles of Narnia*.

The second recommendation from the doctor was to seek somatic counseling to reconnect my mind with my body, and retrain it. In the counseling sessions I learned such things as if I held my shoulders up in a situation of stress instead of keeping them down and relaxed, it would send a signal to my body that something was wrong, reinforcing that hyper-vigilant state.

Finally, the third directive from the doctor was to heal the emotional trauma stored in my body so I could come to a place of complete physical and emotional health. That was and is the hardest part. Though I had been working on my emotional healing for so many years and had believed I was healed, God let me know that yes, I was healed, but that was only one layer. There were many more layers to go. So, my journey to inner healing continued. It is laid out for you to follow in *Walking Tall*, and *Break Forth*, and will be continued in the next book in this series, *Coming Through the Fire*.

It would be nine months from the episode in my classroom until I felt a difference in my health. By January I could work full time again, though I still had to take it easy and could not get involved in much outside of work. The nausea and weakened body were gone, as were the spikes of pain in my head. (Though they do reappear from time to time when I have been overex-

Break Forth

posed to radiation.) I could attend church and different events, but I had to be cautious. My legs no longer gave out on me. I still had the roar in my head at times and I still had the headache, though it was lower in intensity. That part was frustrating, but it was so much easier to handle when all the other symptoms were gone. It would be another nine months until the headache would not be twenty-four/seven, and another six months until the headache only occurred intermittently, with the band around my brain completely gone.

    I still continue to eat healthy, though not quite as stringent. I still struggle with the roar in my head, especially when I lay down at night, and I thankfully only feel it burning or spiking from time to time. I do have to be quite cautious of where I go and how I spend my time. I can no longer feel the electricity and sources of radiation as dramatically as I could for those months, and what I do feel just makes me uncomfortable rather than bringing intense pain. And I can now handle more exposure for longer periods of time before I notice it. It no longer feels like walking into a wall when I enter a building with Wi-Fi! My writing is still done in a journal (pen to paper—I would have it no other way!) but I can type quite a few pages at a time with only mild symptoms. At one point I didn't believe that would even be possible again. I have become my doctor's poster child for healing; especially in regards to emotional healing, yet I am still trusting God for my complete physical and emotional restoration.

    As much as I hated that prophetic word that I had to walk through this health crisis instead of being instantly healed, I understand why it was necessary. It totally turned my life and my understandings upside down. I look back at some parts of that journey with a certain type of fondness—a tenderness or almost sweetness I had never experienced before. I, for the first time in my life, had to treat myself with kid gloves. I could no longer put my head down and push through like I usually did. (There is still a time and a place for that now when God calls me to—but only when He calls me to do it.) I literally had nothing left with which to push through. I was forced to see myself differently, and to not take myself for granted nor take advantage of myself. I had to be cautious and attentive to my every need. I had to take myself off the bottom of my list of priorities and put myself on the top. I had to see myself through eyes of mercy and grace. Basically, I had to see myself as God did. In doing so, I finally and gratefully gained a deeper understanding of how God sees me, and the tender compassion He feels towards me.

From that understanding grew an intimacy with the Lord I never had before. I became solely dependent on Him. I could no longer rely on myself or do things in my strength—I did not have any! I understood to the core of my being, what it meant to honor my body, the temple of the Holy Spirit the Lord gave me. I need to honor it by giving it the rest the Lord calls me to give it. This means saying "No" when I have to, learning to walk in the peace of His presence in all circumstances, and to fight to preserve my physical rest and sleep. I have to put nourishment into my body that will heal and replenish it, rather than choosing foods that will slowly cause it to deteriorate. I need to keep my body fit enough to physically do all the Lord is calling me to do, and strong enough to be the container of the Holy Spirit God wants me to be.

God is calling us to a higher level of purity, free from toxins of all manners, and I believe this is not only in the spiritual realm, but in the natural as well. I have to learn to walk in the peace that is only possible in His constant presence. I also have to keep pursuing my emotional healing by asking God to continue to expose all the areas in which I still need to heal, as painful as that is. I need to remain free of toxic relationships that suck me in and draw too much out of me. If God wants to treat me with loving kindness as His precious treasure, and I need to treat myself tenderly as the daughter of the King that I am, isn't it just as important for those around me to do the same? How is it okay if I then allow someone else in my life to treat me worse than garbage?

Being fairly fit and strong all my life, I did not see the slow damage creeping over my body just from life and choices, and then greatly amplified by my years of abuse and trauma. What happened to my health was a huge shock. But I am so glad it happened as it did, as it came on me so suddenly and so fiercely that I was absolutely forced to make necessary changes in my lifestyle. Had I been healed instantly, I would have gone back to exactly the same way I was living—pushing too hard, omitting things that now I know are crucial—yet believing I was making healthy choices, and not doing too badly. It would have eventually caught up with me again. I believe with all my heart, that had I not made the changes in my lifestyle, or had I chosen the painkillers, I would have eventually succumbed to a life-threatening disease in my body.

So now, dear Reader, it is time to reflect on your lifestyle, and on the choices you have been making that may be affecting your physical, mental, emotional and spiritual health. It is time to pray to heal the trauma your body has endured. Know that unhealed trauma causes many unforeseen problems in not only your mental and emotional state, but in your physical state as well. Come, pray with us and ask the Lord to help you start making the changes He would like you to make, little by little, to bring yourself to complete health. Ask Him to reveal to you what you need to do, and how to do it. Ask Him for strength for this journey, and for Him to help you make it as much a priority as He deems necessary. Ask Him to give you the strength to honor yourself and your body, soul and spirit, the way He does. (Adapt this prayer as necessary.)

Break Forth

Dear Lord,

Thank You that I am fearfully and wonderfully made. Thank You for designing me with the capacity to heal in every area of my being: mentally, emotionally and physically. Father, please help me honestly reflect on the choices I have been making in my lifestyle that may eventually put my health, in any capacity, at risk. Teach me how to honor my body as the temple of the Holy Spirit, as You have created it to be. Show me what this means in my life. Show me where I have not been honoring to You or to myself, and reveal to me the changes I need to make to bring complete health to me—body, mind and emotions. Help me make my health a priority. I ask for the strength and the knowledge to do so.

In all the areas where I have chosen unhealthy measures to cover up pain, comfort myself, relieve tension or hide from the world, all the negative things I do that take the place of coming to You, I lay them at Your feet. Please forgive me for these choices. I ask You to take them, and in their place, help me to seek my comfort only from You. Restore unto me a healthy lifestyle, full of eating right, rest, the right amount of exercise, drinking enough water,

Break Forth

developing healthy relationships with godly people, and spending time in Your presence. I pray I can rest nightly in Your peace. I break off any distractions that prevent me from going to bed on time and allowing me sufficient sleep. I bind up any destructive forces of the enemy that keep me awake at night. Please reveal any unhealthy habits I am following that are preventing the sleep You have ordained. Help me be disciplined in guarding my rest, so I can be strengthened each night. I pray You will instruct my heart as I sleep, and that I will be renewed and restored as each morning breaks. I pray for a peaceful sleep, full of God breathed dreams and visions. Protect me from the schemes of the enemy that try to attack me as I slumber, robbing me of the vitality You have for me.

Thank You that I can cast all my cares on You; that You will take my anxiety and stress and lead me to the answers I need in my life. Thank You that I do not have to carry these things on my own, but You have already won the battle so I can be physically, emotionally and mentally healthy as I keep coming to You for Your grace and healing. For all my specific health issues, I ask for wisdom, revelation and correct information so I understand the whole area, and know Your plan for my healing.

Break Forth

Help me press into my healing so I will learn all You have put forth for me to learn as I travel along this path. Please give me the discipline and determination I need to walk through all that is required for my complete healing.

I pray You bring people across my path to educate me, motivate me and even walk with me. Please help me to have an active lifestyle. Help me fall in love with my body and love feeling it move, stretch and strengthen, just as You created it to do. Lord, I pray You reveal, remove and heal any trauma stored in my body that is making me unwell. I ask for wisdom, guidance and provision to put everything that I will need in place, as I seek after You and Your plan to gain my healing.

Father God, in all honesty, I am struggling in some areas of my life. I am overwhelmed and I can't seem to get ahead, no matter what I try. So I thank You that You are a good Father, and You will hand me the pieces of the puzzle that is my life, one at a time, and show me exactly where they fit, so I can become healthy in every way.

I ask for patience and endurance to walk in a healthy lifestyle. Whether You choose to heal me immediately or gradually, I ask that You help me to make these

Break Forth

changes in my lifestyle so I can maintain my health, and start honoring You and myself, as You have asked of me. Help me to embrace every victory You give me along the way. I thank You, Lord, for giving me the keys to my healing as I come into proper alignment under You—spirit, soul and body. Thank You that as I become closer to You and become more spiritually sound, I also become more mentally, emotionally and physically healthy and whole. Thank You that in Christ, I can truly prosper in spirit, soul and body. I pray this in Your name, Lord Jesus. Amen.

> Don't you realize that your body is the temple of the Holy Spirit, who lives in you and was given to you by God? You do not belong to yourself, for God bought you with a high price.
> So you must honor
> God with your body.
> *1 Corinthians 6:19-20*

Break Forth

> And so, dear brothers and sisters, I plead with you to give your bodies to God because of all he has done for you. Let them be a living and holy sacrifice—the kind he will find acceptable. This is truly the way to worship him.
> *Romans 12:1*

Oh My Child,

Give your hand to Me, and I will lift you up. It is all about trust. Trust that I will make you strong as you ask. Trust Me to heal your body, your mind, as you ask. Trust Me to give you wisdom as you seek it with all your heart. As your heart becomes fully mine, I can do wonderful things in your body, soul and spirit. Many treasures are open to you as you fully place your life and trust in My capable hands. I do not want, and I do not leave you in want. That is not My way. My way is life to the fullest in all capacities of your life. My grace goes ever before you to help you through the learning struggles that await you. But take heart. I am there in them with you, and much will be accomplished through those storms in your life. But My grace will more than get you through. My grace will make you shine. Walk in peace, My love. All is well. All is well.

♥ Jesus

Chapter Fifteen

The Chains of Slavery

When Rachel Hickson, the guest preacher from England, started speaking about the dogs constantly nipping at our heels, I knew she was speaking directly about my situation. It did not matter what I said or did, but here it was six years later, and I was still under Rob's scrutiny and unrelenting vicious attacks. The dog was definitely nipping at my heels. Yet when the altar call came, I did not feel the heart-pounding need to respond like I usually did. I felt nothing—totally indifferent.

But God wanted to heal me, and was not about to let anything stop His plans. He laid it on my friend's heart to take me up for prayer. Though discouraged by another who felt I would know if I was to respond, she was released by Rachel's words, "If you have to get a friend and bring them up, then do it." Strike two came with my own rejection, ensuring her I felt no urge to go. But amidst my protest, she was persistent, as she knew she had to be obedient. Absolutely trusting her connection to the Lord, I finally went.

Break Forth

At first, totally disconnected, I wondered why I was even up at the altar. But as Rachel began praying for those who felt like something was always attacking them, I doubled over—I could not stand up straight. Something was being dug out; dug out from the very depths of my soul. At the same time, one of the leaders from the Cleansing Stream Ministry Team was given a shocking vision of me. She was at the back of the church and suddenly, she later said, it was as if a bright light was shining on me. I was all she could see. She saw that both of my hands and both of my legs were bound by shackles and fitted with heavy chains, like a slave from times past being held in bondage by his master. She knew she was to go pray for me, but listened to God for the when and how.

From my perspective, she just came flying out of nowhere, and though in tears under the power of Holy Spirit, in confidence and authority she started cutting off the spiritual chains keeping me tightly in bondage. The only thing I specifically remember being broken were the chains of doubt. She later said they were on my left hand. It seems like those chains were the key, for they were blocking everything else. Once they were broken, everything else came tumbling off.

God later revealed to me that these chains, had they remained intact, would have kept me in bondage, which would have lead to mental illness. I can see the symptoms of Post Traumatic Stress Disorder (PTSD) scattered throughout my journals, and now in my books. The nightmares, the exaggerated startle reflex, the relentless feeling of impending attack, the sleeplessness, having to be in a safe place to let myself be vulnerable and cry, the numbness and feeling like I lived my life at arm's length with my mind and emotions always detached from my body, among others, are such symptoms.

I would also easily have been a candidate to be labeled and treated with medication for several types of chronic anxiety disorders and depression.

Break Forth

Though I never did cave in to the temptation of cutting my body with a sharp object, one of the ultimate expressions of debilitating pain, the fact that my thoughts were often drawn to it is downright scary from where I now stand.

The symptoms of these mental illnesses cannot help but develop through constant unhealed trauma. Throughout the years of abuse, layer upon layer of trauma had been deposited in my mind and stored in my body, changing my brain chemistry and thought patterns. As these layers piled up, they built a black box in which I had lived, with the ceiling and the walls pushing in on me, smothering every part of me. The black box silenced the voice of God and the voice of reason within me. My prayers bounced off its ceiling. I was very quickly heading to the place where I would have been locked in the prison of my own mind, trapped by the oppressive forces that sought to torment and bind me up so I would stay in the prison they had prepared for me. I would have been held back from walking out my true destiny; distracted and trapped into a life of self-focus, self-doubt and self-preservation. I would have been kept out of walking in the light and love God had intended for me since the beginning of the ages.

But the Lord showed me that though mental illness is real, healing was available. I had to put everything into balance by aligning my body, soul and spirit under God, in the proper order. My top priority was to focus on God, and He would heal the trauma in my mind, the source of the mental illness. Walking through the pain it took was more difficult in the short term than choosing medication that would perhaps make me feel somewhat better. But this was the only way for God to heal my mind.

Had I sought after the alternative road and the label that would have allowed me to accept the lie that I had to live with a mental illness, then I would have been stuck in layer upon layer of filth from the world and from the enemy that had attached itself to my mind. I would never have been able

Break Forth

to live in the total freedom to which God is calling me. God showed me that I could be freed from the lie of the enemy if I constantly washed in the blood of Jesus, and asked Him to renew my mind daily. God's mercies are new every morning, (Lamentations 3:22-23), but the world has become too busy a place to see the real priority of putting Jesus absolutely first. It is essential to allow His spirit to wash over us and cleanse us every day. God gave me a very precise understanding on the importance of this through a dream.

In this dream there was a pornographic picture on a CD cover. It was only a flash, but an attack of the enemy, it clearly was! In prayer, my mentor could see that it had put a spot on my garments of righteousness that otherwise were clean and without wrinkle. That was all it took to mar me—one brief flash of an inappropriate picture in a dream. She saw the spot go as she prayed. This event reinforced my understanding that I had to cleanse myself daily through prayer and time in the Lord's presence. Time with Him washes me clean, body, soul and spirit, but also helps me to recognize when I need to be washed. Without taking time to revel in His word, in His presence, the washing with His blood does not happen. Then, layer upon layer of filth is built up, clogging all outlets that reveal Him to us. When we are so clogged down by this sludge, our mind and body cannot function as they were designed, and disease is the result. But Jesus heals all diseases and all illnesses, which includes mental illness. I believe it does not have to be an accepted part of the Christian life.

In my situation, I had the advantage of a stable foundation of love and support in my family of origin, and of knowing the source of my anxiety and depression was completely environmental. This deflected some of the power of the enemy's attack of mental illness against me, and made my healing somewhat easier. But some people may believe they have always felt a certain way, so they do not recognize its actual origin. Perhaps the trauma

Break Forth

happened when they were too little to remember; and with trauma of one so young and vulnerable, the wounds go deep. Or perhaps it was just the slow build up of unhealed trauma, with each event seemingly insignificant in itself, but with the cumulative effect being deadly. **This disbelief that there is a specific source for the issue leads to the belief in the lie that there is then no cure; it cannot be healed.** They thus believe they have to accept it as part of their life. But that is not the case. Nothing is too big for our God. If you earnestly seek Him, He will reveal the source of unhealed trauma in your life that has overtaken you and has led to mental illness. And then He will show you the path to complete healing.

I received great release that day at the altar, and became so much closer in my quest for complete freedom. It was no wonder the enemy so clearly tried to block the prayer ministry slated to happen that day. He did not want me coming out from the chains of doubt, and the bondage of mental illness that had me shackled and bound into a future of slavery. God will still bring to mind that event, and remind me the chains are gone—the only thing holding me is that which I put on myself. I thank God for my friend who heard the voice of the Lord for me, when I could not.

Now, dear Reader, the light is shining brightly on you. God wants to break off all the chains in your life that are holding you in slavery in your body and in your mind. He wants to reveal the lies you may be holding in your life as truth. Though they may be true in the world, you are not of the world, and the Lord is above all of it. Believe in His truth for your life, not the truth of this world. He can heal your trauma. He can free you from all chains, and lead you to the freedom you can feel deep in your heart, clamoring to get out and be felt. He wants you to fly. And you can. Let's pray.

Break Forth

Father God,

Thank You, that I can come to You for everything. I thank You that You know me so well in every area—spiritually, mentally, emotionally, physically. You know what I need and what needs to be healed so I can be healthy and whole in every one of those areas. Thank You for not wanting to leave me the same way You found me, but wanting to heal every part of me, in every way.

Father God, please open my eyes, soften my heart, and show me the areas of my life where I need to release and repent for actions I have taken, words I have spoken and thoughts I have had that have brought hurt into my life and into the lives of people around me. (Ask Holy Spirit to show you anything you need to confess before the Father, and anyone you need to forgive. Then continue on to the next section where you will be led in repentance and forgiveness.)

Right now I bind up the accuser, who loves to come and assign shackles against each one of us. He tries to find areas where he can tighten the bar on our wrists and feet and pin it down, leaving us enslaved.

Break Forth

But Father, I loose and break all the chains and shackles on me right now by the authority of Jesus Christ, and the power of the finished work of the cross. I take authority over them right now by taking a strong stand and repenting and renouncing the sins of _____. Father, I confess those sins to You and ask for Your forgiveness. I also bring _____ before You. I choose to forgive them. Do not hold them guilty on my account, but bless them.

Lord God, for any area I have chosen to walk in disobedience away from You, I ask forgiveness. I now break off the weight, power and authority of any of the chains assigned against me from any source, in Jesus' name.

Lord God, if there is an access point for the enemy generationally, where he has gained authority to come in and entangle me through my mother's or father's bloodline, I break that off right now in Jesus' name. I repent on behalf of those who came in generations before me, for all the sin in my family line.

Lord God, in Jesus' name, I break off any word curses or vows spoken over me, or that I have claimed to be true in my life. I break off any lies the enemy has spoken over me, accusing me of not being good enough,

Break Forth

that I will not succeed, that I will not be healed, that I am crazy, that I have to live with mental illness, or the lie that _____.

Lord God, I trust that You want me to be free, so in any area I have not forgiven myself, or released unto You; any area I am still hanging on to that keeps me in bondage, I pray You show me and help me release it into Your hands. Forgive me for not trusting You with that area of my life. Show me how to be totally free from any form of mental illness and bondage, Lord. Holy spirit, in every area that You break a chain holding me back, cover that area with the spirit of love, power, authority and a clear and sound mind.

As You break the chains, Lord Jesus, show me how to move forward. Show me how I can become a chain breaker through the power of Holy Spirit. Teach me how to reach out and touch others, teach others and take on the authority You have given us to set other people free. I want to have an impact in Your Kingdom, Lord. I thank You for desiring for me to become free, because the more free I am, the more impact I can have on others, showing them the way to freedom.

Father God, I come against any spirits of desolation, despair, failure, rejection and hopelessness.

Break Forth

I bind up these forces coming against me, and cast them out in Jesus' name. I will not partner with them in my life. Lord Jesus, You are my hope; with You I am no longer lost. In You, the Father sees me as perfect, worthy, and righteous. Fill me with Your hope, acceptance, love and encouragement. Help me see others and myself as You see us.

Father God, You give us new life and victory as the chains that have been enslaving us are broken. You fill us with hope. Thank You that hope restored is the abundance of life. Thank You for taking me out of a desolate, black season, changing me and placing me in Your spring time, with flowers of new life coming forth all around me. Thank You for restoring my energy, faith, and belief that I am worth fighting for, and that those around me are worth fighting for. Lord God, thank You for giving me a healthy thought life and healthy habits so I can stay free from bondage, and live in the hope that You have promised me. Help me draw near to You. Teach me how to live continually in Your presence, Lord. Thank You for Your peace. I pray this in Jesus' name. Amen.

Break Forth

> I cried out, "I am slipping!" but your unfailing love, O LORD, supported me. When doubts filled my mind, your comfort gave me renewed hope and cheer.
> *Psalm 94:18-19*

> I will bless my people and their homes around my holy hill. And in the proper season I will send the showers they need. There will be showers of blessing. The orchards and fields of my people will yield bumper crops, and everyone will live in safety. When I have broken their chains of slavery and rescued them from those who enslaved them, then they will know that I am the LORD.
> *Ezekiel 34:26-27*

> Now I will break the yoke of bondage from your neck and tear off the chains of Assyrian oppression.
> *Nahum 1:13*

Break Forth

Dear Child,

There is hope and peace in a journey with Me despite outwcircumstances. Stand strong in all you do. Stand for all you do. I am calling you forth so I will direct your path. You are no longer bound by the chains of doubt. It is the belief that set you free. It sets you free to rise up and act on My behalf. I will call you out now and have you act and speak on My behalf. I will give you the words as you need them. I will guide you. As I have restored you, I will keep pouring out of you. You are My story. I have healed you and now you are free … free to worship Me … free to live in the peace I call you to have. I am calling it all forth now. You are free. You have been set free by My power, by My love, by My hope. A new joy is bubbling up out of your heart—your very soul—and your mind will follow. Keep obedient to Me. Keep a soft heart. Keep a humble heart, and I will keep pouring out of you and spill over into others. Your journey begins, My child! Hang on! It is going to be quite a ride!

♥ Jesus

Chapter Sixteen

God's Protection

I REMEMBER HIM STANDING IN THE HALLWAY OF THE HOUSE I LIVED IN with my parents. I must have been about twenty years old at the time. He was picking me up for a date. I don't remember his name, and now I even question that the one he gave me was real. He was looking at the pictures on the wall of me, of Jesus, and of various scripture verses. At the time, I thought that night was very strange, but I never really dwelled on it until God revealed the truth of it many years later.

I had met him on the plane. He seemed nice, was well dressed and clean cut. We chatted throughout the flight. I had no misgivings about going out on a date with him when he requested it. As we drove away from the bright lights of the city, the stars became more visible as they danced across the heavens. It was quiet and peaceful in the abandoned farmyard where we had just stopped for what I had thought was to gaze at them ... but almost immediately, he went back into the car without an explanation. Puzzled, I did the same. Driving back to the city, not one word was spoken. He let me out of the car in front of my house, still without a word, and drove off.

Though I was disappointed and incredibly confused about the date that never was, it did not have a lasting impact on me, and life carried on as normal. There had never been a moment that night or in my memory where I had felt the slightest bit of suspicion or fear. But almost thirty years later, God would bring that long forgotten night to remembrance and reveal what this man's true intentions had been. The plan had been to rape me, of that I know. Whether he would have left me, bloody and battered, to find my way home, or if I would have become a face on a poster—my family frantic in their search for me—that I do not know.

The revelation makes sense to me. There really is no other reasonable explanation for the strange behavior of that night. I was shocked, as the truth of what could have ... should have happened to me hit my heart. There is also no other reasonable explanation as to why he just stopped, or changed his mind; no other explanation than the incredible fact of God's sovereign protection. God protected me. I should have been raped and possibly murdered, but God protected me. A life-changing (or ending) event should have happened, but that was not my story, that was not to be my story, so God abruptly stopped it. God has also protected me in other ways throughout my life, and definitely in my marriage. Sometimes we are aware of the things from which God has protected us. But there are other times in which we are totally unaware of how God has been our shield, until He reveals it in amazing ways. The following account is one such revelation.

Break Forth

Battle Scars

I've always known I carry a lot of emotional scars. Deep wounds are inflicted when you are cut to the core of your soul time and time again. Even though these wounds heal, they do leave their mark. But, I never would have believed someone would see my scars. Nor did I understand what a calculated attack it was that put them there, or how deeply God's protection covered me. The process of this revelation stunned me, and it has had an everlasting impact on who I was, and who I was to become.

One evening after a particularly challenging week, I met with two of my amazing prophetic friends for prayer. At one point as they were praying for me, I happened to lean forward. As I did, one of my friends let out a loud, emotional cry and became visibly shaken. I heard her whisper something about scars to our other friend. I asked her what it was. All she could say was, "I see your scars." She was crying and was too emotional, even afterward, to speak about it.

The next week I asked her about it again. I wanted to know more about my scars. I wanted to know what they looked like. For some reason, it was so very important for me to know all about them. They were part of me, and a testament to what I had endured. She began to weep again, and was still not ready to talk about it. At that point, I realized what an honor it was for me that God had chosen to show my scars to someone. It obviously had a dramatic impact on her. Somehow it provided validation of the pain of all I had survived.

I carry no physical scars from my years of trauma. To look at me now, no one would even suspect all the emotional damage that had been inflicted upon me. There is nothing to tell the tale of the hell I had walked through. I chose not to share it with many. Only my closest friends and some

Break Forth

of my family knew somewhat of my past. And even they did not know the magnitude of my woundedness. But now God had shown someone my pain; the true depths of the pain I bore all those years. Somehow that revelation made the burden I still carry, a little easier. My battle scars were real.

A little while later, my friend told me that the scars run across the flat of my back from the top of my shoulder down to the end of my back. She wrote this letter describing them, and gave me the scriptures to go with it:

> Calli:
>
> When you leaned over for us to pray for you that night, I saw scars, the scars on your back. In fact, I still see them in my mind's eye. They haven't faded. I looked up pictures of scars to show you what I see, but none of them were like the ones I see on you.
>
> Yours are silvery white. This is good because they are no longer red and inflamed. They are about half an inch thick and they are evenly spaced. I've tried to count them, but got emotional when I do.
>
> Because I was so stricken when I first saw them that I couldn't talk or write about it. I knew there was more so I've been praying about it.
>
> The scars that you bear are the result of strategically placed strikes that were done with evil intent. The person who was used is a pawn in the enemy's hand. Lord have mercy on this one

Break Forth

Psalm 10:17-18 (NKJV)

You, LORD, hear the desire of the afflicted; you encourage them and you listen to their cry, defending the fatherless and the oppressed, so that mere earthly mortals will never again strike terror.

Psalm 18: 1-6, 16-17

I love you, LORD, my strength. The LORD is my rock, my fortress and my deliverer; my God is my rock, in whom I take refuge, my shield and the horn of my salvation, my stronghold. I called to the LORD, who is worthy of praise, and I have been saved from my enemies. The cords of death entangled me; the torrents of destruction overwhelmed me. The cords of the grave coiled around me; the snares of death confronted me. In my distress I called to the LORD; I cried to my God for help. From his temple he heard my voice; my cry came before him, into his ears.

He reached down from on high and took hold of me; he drew me out of deep waters. He rescued me from my powerful enemy, from my foes, who were too strong for me.

In the next few days, the Lord again honored me by speaking to my spirit, teaching me about my scars. He told me I had earned my stripes, and that they made me well seasoned and strong. He shared with me that I had survived a strategic battle designed to destroy me, but He pulled me out of that and raised me up for great and mighty things. I knew these stripes gave

Break Forth

me confidence, since I had already survived the deadly battle with the enemy, and would continue to be victorious as I walked with the Lord.

At first, I was unsettled as I realized the brutal attacks from the pit of hell I had experienced were, in fact, literally designed to take me out—and they were intentional. It was not an overly fun realization. But God settled my heart when I finally understood that He had specifically protected and saved me, and that I was now healed from it! If He could protect me all those years from an *in house* attack, He can protect me from anything, in every situation, and in every circumstance. I could, indeed, trust Him with my life—and I do.

This experience was powerful. I was humbled and honored. It forged in my spirit a new level of trust and understanding of who God is—my strength and shield, my Savior and fortress, my rock in whom I find protection, the power that saved me, my place of safety. These were no longer just words to me. I was able to repent for my bad attitudes toward Rob—my part in it. (Yes, this is an ongoing prayer!) I asked the Lord to help me treat him with love and honor. Some days I am successful in it and others ... not so much. My heart was set free that day, knowing I am under His protection.

At this time in your life, dear Reader, you may not see your own deep wounds that need healing. You may not even know what wounds and scars you carry. But they are impacting your life and making your heart heavy. They affect how you see the world. They affect the decisions and the choices you make. They affect your relationships, or lack thereof. These wounds even affect who God is to you and the depth of your trust relationship with Him.

No, you may not see them or know all that are there, but God does. He sees them all. He knows them all. And He desires to heal you. He desires to raise you up to do great and mighty things in His Kingdom. He wants to develop an understanding within you of how He has protected you and how He will continue to protect you. He wants to forge within you strength be-

Break Forth

yond human reason that will allow you to walk out your God given destiny, in full confidence of His protection. The Lord Jesus Christ understands our pain and our stripes. He bore His own so we can be healed. "By his stripes we are healed" (Isaiah 53:5 NKJV). Now we will stand with you as you turn to the Lord and pray, so you too, can be healed and protected, and BREAK FORTH into the destiny God has for you.

> Dear Lord of Heaven's Armies,
>
> I thank You that You are my protector and cornerstone, and that You won total victory at Calvary. I ask for a new, deeper revelation of the true power and might of the cross and of Your blood. Lord, Your word says You are close to the brokenhearted. I am one of the brokenhearted ones, so I choose to believe You are close to me. Please bring truth to all the situations in my life where You protected me, and where I feel You didn't protect me, so I may be set free.
>
> I ask You to reveal and break off the things in my life I am doing to protect myself, including any parts of my personality I have created to keep myself safe, instead of allowing and trusting You to protect me. Please heal all fear, terror and trauma in me that will prevent me from letting go of these protective personalities. Help me to let my guard down and be vulnerable so You can bring healing.

Break Forth

Read through the list of common protective personalities, noticing which ones resonate within your spirit.

Doormat	Blank
Confusion	Anger
The Protector	Invisible
I'm ok	The Wall
Numb	Overwhelmed
Control	Independence
The Bully	The Victim
The Martyr	The Perfectionist
Needy	Nice
The Phony	The Pleaser
Over Achiever	The Critic
Don't mess with me	Rescuer

*Ask Holy Spirit what the job of this protective personality is, and how you believe it has kept you safe. Thank this protective personality for guarding you, and then release it, proclaiming that now Jesus will protect you instead.

From the Genesis Process 10
(Used with permission)

Break Forth

Help me to be strong, Lord, yet soft before You. I know I do not have to be tough any longer, as You will protect me. I pray You root out any spirit of condemnation keeping me in bondage and making me feel unprotected and at fault for the things that have happened to me. Rip off the veil covering my face that the enemy has put on me to darken my mind. Take off the blinders covering my eyes, so I can see You as my protector, and so I can see where You were in each of the scary situations in my life. I pray You shine the light so I can see Your hand in every situation; I want to see how You brought me through it, and how You are going to change it around so it works out for my good.

I know sometimes, Father, I just see the muck and the ugliness in front of me, but You see everything behind the scenes. You see the canvas being painted. You see the metal being purified. You see the sword being forged—while I just see the pain. Help me to trust Your goodness, Lord, in all the events in my life, even the ones I don't understand. Help me believe all of it will work together for the good, to forge me into the strong warrior You are calling me to be.

I ask You, Father, to heal all the memories of every harmful thing that has come into my life; every form of mental, physical, emotional, sexual and spiritual abuse.

Break Forth

Please, Lord, come and heal them now, in Jesus' name. Please show me where You were in each memory, for I choose to believe that when I see You there, I will be healed and gain victory so I can walk from glory to glory. [Take time now to ask God, by the power of Holy Spirit, to reveal a memory that needs to be healed. Ask Jesus to show you how He was with you in this event. Look into His face and see His heart toward you. Then ask Him to heal the memory. You may need to do this several times for different memories. Come back to this prayer as often as the Lord directs you.]

Dear Lord, thank You for reaching down from on high, taking hold of me, and drawing me out of deep waters. Thank You for rescuing me from my enemies, who were too strong for me. I know You have started a good work in me, and You will continue it right to the end. Lord, I am done being one of the voiceless ones. Help me to stand up for not only myself, but for other women and children, and for the men in my same situation.

Lord, lift my chin, and help me to start speaking out in answer to Your call to literally change the world, in Jesus' name. I know, Lord, that whatever situations we have victory in we have authority over, so I receive that new authority in Christ, under His ultimate protection.

Break Forth

> Please show me the next steps for my life, Lord, and help me walk them in God-confidence instead of fear, knowing You are protecting me. In Your strength I can break forth into victory, taking ground and chasing back the enemy. I choose to move forward into my inheritance in Your authority. Make me a protector of Your Word, Your land and Your children. Please give me love for Your people and a sound mind to do Your will. Amen

My prayer team prays this over you:

For you who were abused as children, we pray the Lord would come and wrap His loving arms around you, and show you His love. We pray you hear Holy Spirit whisper to your heart, "It's not your fault." We pray this will set you free. We break off any lies of blame. As the mighty Army of Christ, we stand up against these lies, and we put the blood of Christ and the cross between you and any spirits spewing lies on you. Like a mighty wall we stand against the accusations of the enemy on your behalf and declare you free. When you feel too wounded to raise your head, let alone your hand, and when you cannot stand any longer, we pray for you to have a personal touch from the Lord. This personal touch will never hurt you, only heal you, and then you'll be amazed how your head will be lifted, and you too, will be able to stand up for others, in God, with a heart full of compassion and a soul full of fire.

Break Forth

We pray that where the scars are, Holy Spirit will bring His salve and healing oil to be poured over you. We pray healing waters to flow over your body. We pray rest comes to you, so you can lay down in the green pastures the Lord brings you to, and experience the grace, mercy and peace of God. He is the good shepherd, and He will take care of you, in Jesus' name.

> "I will make a covenant of peace with my people and drive away the dangerous animals from the land. Then they will be able to camp safely in the wildest places and sleep in the woods without fear.
> *Ezekiel 34:25*

> The LORD is my shepherd; I have all that I need. He lets me rest in green meadows; he leads me beside peaceful streams. He renews my strength. He guides me along right paths, bringing honor to his name. Even when I walk through the darkest valley, I will not be afraid, for you are close beside me. Your rod and your staff protect and comfort me. You prepare a feast for me in the presence of my enemies. You honor me by anointing my head with oil. My cup overflows with blessings.
> *Psalm 23:1-5*

Break Forth

And through your faith, God is protecting you by his power until you receive this salvation, which is ready to be revealed on the last day for all to see. So be truly glad. There is wonderful joy ahead, even though you have to endure many trials for a little while. These trials will show that your faith is genuine. It is being tested as fire tests and purifies gold—though your faith is far more precious than mere gold. So when your faith remains strong through many trials, it will bring you much praise and glory and honor on the day when Jesus Christ is revealed to the whole world. You love him even though you have never seen him. Though you do not see him now, you trust him; and you rejoice with a glorious, inexpressible joy.

1 Peter 1:5-8

Break Forth

My heart is with you, Child.

    You flow in My peace now. My presence goes with you in all you say and do. Honor Me. Honor My name. Walk tall in the honor that has been bestowed on you. My healing grace still flows through you; floods your heart, mind and soul. Revel in its power. Revel in its strength and glory. Let it flow out of you and into other people's lives. Honor them. Honor My people. Let them know I love them. Let grace and mercy flow out of your heart to touch lives. I am calling you up to a high purpose. Now you are ready. I will set things in motion as you keep seeking My face. Rest and trust in Me. Keep putting all things before Me to do with as I will. The peace is evident in you. Keep walking in it. Let it shine forth. Walk in the freedom I have given you. Heaven is open over you. Watch it pour out!

                                                                 ♥ Jesus

Chapter Seventeen

The Gift of Struggle

The attacks came full force that night, once again trying to strip me bare of all dignity and value. His words were meaner than ever before, and the accusation more seething and outrageous. Afterward, I cried out to the Lord, raw and vulnerable, telling Him how broken I was. After eight years apart, this assault was still as ferocious as ever. I felt I could no longer go on with this continuous tearing of my soul. I wanted to crumble, to cave in. I was seeking comfort from the Lord. But God was instead seeking to give me a spiritual upgrade. Out of my pen poured the words inspired by the Lord:

Break Forth

Stand up strong and be the warrior I am calling you to be. Pay him no mind! All you need is Me. Focus on Me. Do My will. Live your life in the way I am calling you to live. You are no longer of the world. Don't expect to be like one of the world! Rise above! This is your testing ground! Are you going to cave in and give up? Who are you? Who am I making you to be? You are loved by many. Do not believe you have not walked in love. I love you so deeply. Rise up in joy! Put the past behind you! How will you react? Who are you, Calli? Who do you believe yourself to be? Who are you in Me? Find your identity in Me, not in who others say you are! Show others your song! Sing it loud! Rise up! Rise up! I know who you are. You know who you are. Stop defending yourself. I am your defender. I will show him when the time is right.

♥ Jesus

Break Forth

At first, I thought I had dismally failed the test. Once again, after all these years, I still engaged in the battle directly with Rob. I still tried to use reason, to use logic, to defend. But at God's word calling me up to a higher spiritual level, I immediately turned to Him in worship. I let every vicious word jumping around in my brain melt away from my mind and heart. I took my eyes off everything but Jesus, and let my heart unfold to meet Him and be touched. As I did, I felt as if the armor and shield of God that continually surrounded me was being fortified many times over. It was as if the text I had received from my friend the previous December was coming to pass as I sat in His presence:

> In the night I was interceding for you and I sensed that the Lord is making your shield thicker/stronger. I could hear the arrows hit it. They made a loud sound so they are strong, but they'd fall because your shield is stronger.

Maybe I had not failed in all facets. By turning to God in worship instead of continuing to wallow, I had now come to the place where I knew I withstood another brutal attack of the enemy meant to destroy my walk of destiny with the Lord. Instead of those arrows denting or breaking through, those darts of the enemy (through Rob's words) caused my shield of faith to be strengthened and reinforced, ready and able to deflect even more than ever before. I was even able to stand up against the enemy and shout out declarations, sending him forcefully off my life. I came to realize that in the attack, God was being God, Rob was being Rob (the injured version of himself) and the enemy was being the enemy. I was, in fact, the only one not being who I truly was.

I have learned the hard way that every problem placed before you, whether by God or by the enemy, can lead to a spiritual upgrade. In every hard situation, we need to start by turning it on its head. Instead of feeling attacked or receiving an attack, we need to start looking at it from various angles, with all the excitement an opportunity for learning, advancement and growth provides us. The most glaring example of this in my life was when I no longer had my health.

When I first realized how serious the illness was that I faced, (as described in "Just Another Chapter"), I admittedly looked for sympathy from those close to my heart in whom I confided. I was definitely given adequate condolences and well wishes from all—all except two. Yet it was their words I will always remember—their words I came to treasure.

These two mighty women of God, having been through the toughest trials in life, shocked me by their responses at the time. As I poured out my woes with tears, they became excited about what God was going to do in my life. Though in separate places at separate times, they each cheered me on, thrilled that God was calling me up to join them in the higher ranks of God's army. Though it was so hard to swallow with no understanding of the gift of struggle, I remained un-offended (though edged with anger and confusion), as I knew they cared about me, and each had experience in tragedy that I had not born.

As I trudged through those months of healing, I slowly began to understand their perspective. God was unraveling this mystery for me: He was taking me to a new spiritual dimension—plain and simple. And this struggle was providing the refinement and depth I needed that could not be accomplished in any other way. He was about to unfold something incredible in my

Break Forth

life, and to do so, He needed me to be wholly dependent on Him and drawing my strength solely from the intimacy I had with Him, rather than from my own willpower and resources. In that time, He set up the foundations I needed to walk out the path He had placed me on before the ages.

So now, when the struggles inevitably come, I see them in a new light. I still sometimes catch myself briefly rolling my eyes at God, breathing a heavy sigh, and suggesting that perchance I had already learned enough!? But then I settle in and ask Him where He is taking me on this adventure, and what amazing thing is He going to do in my life with this gift. I ask Him what part of my heart needs refining, what part of my character is going to start shining in a new way, or what miracle am I going to watch unfold before my very eyes. I ask Him what wisdom and knowledge is He imparting to me with this gift of struggle, and how am I going to pass it on to His other ones that need to know its profound value.

I have come a long way in my outlook on life. Admittedly, it is much more glorious looking down at my life from the mountaintop I now stand on with my God. But know, dear Reader, I still understand deeply what it feels like to look up at the steep climb ahead, cringing, and wondering if it will ever end. But I am here to tell you that yes, there is hope. Every struggle over which you become victorious places a depth of character in your heart, a revelation in your soul and a key in your spirit that will eventually step out and be known. It will all suddenly make sense—everything you have been through—well, most of it. And you too, will be utterly amazed at what God can now do in your life. Come. Let us pray, and then go open that present together.

Break Forth

Lord God,

I enter Your courts with thanksgiving and praise, knowing You are a good God. You are a just God and You will do what You need to do, and it is not for me to say, it is only for me to trust. As I come through this valley time of struggle, though it is hard, I know it is where I will grow and flourish the most. As I look up to the mountain ahead of me I must climb, help me not get overwhelmed. Help me focus on You in this journey. Thank You that Your glory radiates and shines on me, making me more like You, Jesus, shiny and polished in new areas of my life, so I can walk forward in the new giftings You have for me.

In every place the enemy has wounded me and robbed me of my giftings, I pray that as I push through the darkness of the valley toward that mountain, continuing to give You praise and practicing thankfulness, You will release and activate each and every gift, known and unknown, that You have for me, in the name of Jesus. Please release every plan and purpose You have for my life. Make me the warrior You have called me to be, ever watchful, and ready to fight in every battle to which You call me. Thank You for all the new weapons of warfare You are bestowing upon me with this journey.

Break Forth

Thank You for strengthening my armor and shield daily so they deflect every fiery dart of the enemy, every word of accusation, every word of hate, every hurt, every other tactic of the enemy. Thank You, Lord, for the helmet of salvation. Thank You that You came to save. Keep that helmet placed firmly on my head, protecting and renewing my mind daily, and helping me to immediately reject every lie of the enemy, before it has a chance to take root. Thank You for the breastplate of righteousness that makes me worthy in Your sight, because of what You have done for me. Thank You for giving me everything I need to stand firm in Your army, shoulder to shoulder with my brothers and sisters in Christ, able to take back ground from the enemy.

Lord, please keep my heart soft and as fertile soil, so that Your Word and Your seeds will be planted deep within it, and bear much fruit. Thank You, God, that You have heard my cries. Thank You for providing for my needs according to Your glorious riches in Christ Jesus. Thank You for giving me the strength I need for this journey.

Lord, I seek truth. I thank You for Your truth. I thank You that I can stand in Your truth. I pray You will grow my trust and as the trust grows, my obedience will continue to grow. I pray that my relationship with You will also deepen and become more intimate as I walk through this valley and learn to trust You more and more.

Break Forth

Thank You that I can climb the mountain with You leading, and there will be great gifts and joy along the way; joy in things I can't even imagine. I am not alone on my journey, and I thank You for that. Though it is dark, the light is coming. Thank You that You are the light.

Lord, I know that when I am through this valley of darkness and up on the mountain top, there will be gifts waiting for me. I receive them all, with the faith of a child. Help me jump in and unwrap the gifts with the exuberance and excitement of a child, ripping open the paper and getting into them, using them, enjoying them, and letting them take me exactly where You want me to be. Thank You, Lord, for these gifts, all sent with love. Thank You for these gifts of love.

> For the angel of the LORD is a guard;
> he surrounds and defends all who fear him.
> *Psalm 34:7*

Break Forth

> Leave him alone and let him curse,
> for the LORD has told him to do it.
> And perhaps the LORD will see that
> I am being wronged and will bless me
> because of these curses today.
> *2 Samuel 16:11-12*

> Commit everything you do to the LORD,
> Trust him, and he will help you.
> He will make your innocence
> radiate like the dawn,
> and the justice of your cause
> will shine like the noonday sun.
> *Psalm 37:5-6*

> For our present troubles are small and won't last very long. Yet they produce for us a glory that vastly outweighs them and will last forever! So we don't look at the troubles we can see now; rather, we fix our gaze on things that cannot be seen. For the things we see now will soon be gone, but the things we cannot see will last forever.
> *2 Corinthians 4:17-18*

Break Forth

> Dear brothers and sisters, when troubles of any kind come your way, consider it an opportunity for great joy. For you know that when your faith is tested, your endurance has a chance to grow. So let it grow, for when your endurance is fully developed, you will be perfect and complete, needing nothing.
> *James 1:2-4*

Dear Child,

Excitement grows in you and fills your tummy. You know there is more. You feel it. You feel Me. You feel My breath on you. Breathe it in. I want you to press into Me. I will lead and guide you as always. Angels are being sent to you to help you. You will find them as you call on Me. My heart extends to you. Look to Me to find your strength. I am your shield. Learn to wield it. Let it protect you. Be strong in it. Protect others with it. Show them how to use My sword and My shield. Pray as you walk. Pray as you work. Fill yourself to overflowing with Me. Then you will overflow. When you are filled to overflowing, then you will have more of My power. You will spill out to others. You are not overflowing yet. You need more of Me.

♥ Jesus

Appendix 1

(This is the second newspaper article I wrote in support of a campaign to financially support shelters for women and children in domestic abuse situations. The editor supplied the title for the article.)

December 2011

Abuse Survivor Admits Journey Still an Uphill Battle

"It was her story. She didn't write it. But she may as well have. She lived it." Powerful words. It makes me start to think about that same article again ... It's been a while since I've read it ... even longer since I had written it. And now its words are quietly provoking me to take my stand, perhaps give a voice to one more woman in a desperate situation; to let her know there is hope; to encourage her that there **is** another way of life...

It is still hard. I will not pretend otherwise. The journey is still an uphill battle, but it no longer *rages*. There are still wounds, and the scars are still there ... but within those scars, there is a strength and a hope ... they provide a constant reminder that I cannot go back. I choose, Yes, **I choose** to not live in a place of raw pain, a place where it feels that every breath is a struggle, a place where you truly do not know how you are going to make it through the day, and worse yet, through the night. I no longer dread the check-out stand at the grocery store, where inevitably the cashier would ask, "How are you today?" and I would have to look away, and fight the tears that question would evoke. It would take everything inside of me to keep it all

Break Forth

together, so I'd put on my mask that helped me to keep it all together, and smile, and lie, and say, "I'm fine ... "

Yet the fights of the night would be rewinding through my mind, and I'd think ... *What I'd really like to scream is that I AM NOT OKAY... when I get home I want to be greeted with a smile in place of the hate that cuts deep into my soul ... I want to live with no fear, and to not be scared to feel or to believe or to hope; all the normal things of life that had become dreams for me in my fragile world of illusion ...* and I'd lie again as I walked away and said, "Yes, I'll have a good day ... "

Yet all I wanted to do was smash the mask that hides the pain and stop the lies that had become my life, leaving me with a mind that could not think, a heart that could not feel, and a spirit where the light could not shine. But that was the life that had become mine ... So now I choose another life ...

The battles are still there, but they are less intense, and less often. And now I can walk away a little easier. I still feel the fear creeping in, in the aftermath of a verbal attack, and I close the blinds and unplug the phones, and pray. But God has put amazing people in my life that help me to hold the line, and help to hold me up when I am shaken. But now it is only shaken, not shattered.

I used to think there was no win, there was no hope, there was no happy ending ... But now I have had some healing, and feel some measure of peace, of joy, of hope. I am proud of the person my journey has forced me to become. And so to you, my sister, my friend, still in the fight, and can't see the way out, I just want to let you know that we are standing by your side, heart to heart, and will help you fight your battle, if only you will let us ... and that we care ... and that we understand ...

Thank you for giving me a voice ... thank you for providing a way, and a hope ...

A Final Word

There is a peace in you now. My peace. By walking through what you had to walk through, facing it, you have victory. You are walking in victory. Gone are the hauntings of the past. Gone are the fears, the unrest, the anxiousness, the mistrust. Complete freedom and trust are yours as you keep walking with Me and trusting on Me. I have much more to show you. Stay open to Me. I am opening heaven up over you. Be watchful. Stay open. Be attuned to My voice. Feel the peace that flows out of you. Others will see it too, and be drawn to it. It is My ministry for you—a ministry of giving peace beyond what they know, to those who also have been trapped by fear and circumstances. Teach them to turn to Me. Teach them to rely on Me. Teach them to see Me in their walk. Help them walk with Me. Help them know that all is not lost. There is so much restoration that can be done as they learn to turn their hearts, their whole hearts, toward Me. Find every missing piece, and free it by giving it over to Me. Show them how. Show them what you have learned and are still learning. Show them how to rest deeply in Me. There is so much hope and peace for all who seek Me. It is yours. Be free. Walk in freedom.

♥ Jesus

Break Forth

This was the commission God gave me for my book series, before I even knew I was writing a book. What you receive victory over, you are given authority in. As you receive your healing and gain victory in this area, you too, will be given authority to set others free from the same captivity in which you were once held. So this, dear Reader, becomes your commission as well. Welcome to the fight on the front line. Hang on tight! It is an amazing ride.

For the glory of God

♥ Calli J. Linwood

> *He rescues the poor from the cutting words of the strong, and rescues them from the clutches of the powerful. And so at last the poor have hope, and the snapping jaws of the wicked are shut.*
> *Job 5:15-16*

End Notes and Resources

1. Linwood, Calli. *Walking Tall*. Helena: Ahelia Publishing Inc, 2015.

2. Tyler-Thompson, Laura Lynn. *Relentless Redemption*. Tulsa: Harrison House, 2013.

3. Cooke, Graham. *Seeing in the Spirit*. Vancouver: Brilliant Book House, 2013.

4. Young, Sarah. *Jesus Calling*. Nashville: Thomas Nelson, 2011.

5. Russell, A.J. (Editor). *God Calling*. Grand Rapids: Fleming H. Revell, 2007.

6. Cleansing Stream Ministries www.cleansingstream.ca

7. Hearts on Fire Ministries www.heartsonfireministries.ca/

8. Levine, Peter. *Waking The Tiger*. Berkeley: North Atlantic Books, 1997.

9. Ober, Sinatra, Zucker. *Earthing – The most important health discovery ever?* Laguna Beach: Basic Health Publications, 2010.

10. The Genesis Process www.genesisprocess.org

> No manna appeared on the day they first ate from the crops of the land, and it was never seen again. So from that time on the Israelites ate from the crops of Canaan.
>
> *Joshua 5:12*

Coming soon ...

Coming Through the Fire

Calli J. Linwood

Shock hit me as, driving to house church none-the-less, various sordid images were suddenly being downloaded into my mind and flashing before my eyes—absolutely random and unprovoked. Fierce horror jumped in and dread filled my soul. *Oh no, no, no, no! Lord! Not that!* It was more than just this current assault that tormented me ... for by now I understood God had mandated me to write and share my story ... and I undoubtedly knew that this too, would eventually be part of it. I would be asked once again to put on a

Break Forth

cloak of humility and expose all my ugliness so the Lord could bring healing to others. *Not my will but Yours, Lord.*

　　I immediately went to my house church leader and received prayer to wash and cleanse me from the images and their impact. It wouldn't be the first time nor the last I would receive prayer for this area; it was just another layer of purification required of me by the Lord. Now that we are both over the shock that the Lord is having me write on this area … let me start at the beginning.

About The Author

A sliver of hope was all Calli J. Linwood had in her soul as she made the hard decisions that would forever change her. As the Lord transformed her life from ashes to beauty, He asked her to record her journey—all of it—the ugly and the magnificent, the raw pain and the joy. Right from the start of her healing, He said her journey was for sharing: "The making of a warrior is a marvelous thing!"

Sharing her story is how she was to link arms with others, far and near, to walk together along the same path; one that would lead out from the muddy trenches to set their feet on high places. Welcome to the journey of a lifetime.

Calli has two amazing children. She holds a Master's Degree in Education, and this is her second book on healing and walking in freedom. She serves on the inner healing and prophetic ministry teams in her local church. Her desire is to partner with the Lord in building His mighty army. She is excited to see the captives set free and deepen their intimate relationship with Jesus.

Break Forth

Break Forth

CPSIA information can be obtained
at www.ICGtesting.com
Printed in the USA
FFOW01n2259200517
35776FF